BLOOD FOR BLOOD

BLOOD FOR BLOOD

THE BLACK AND TAN WAR IN GALWAY

William Henry

MERCIER PRESS

IRISH PUBLISHER – IRISH STORY

For Peg Broderick and Uncle Ollie,
and Grandad William Henry

MERCIER PRESS

Cork

www.mercierpress.ie

© William Henry, 2012

© Preface: Joe Connolly, 2012

ISBN: 978 1 78117 046 5

10 9 8 7 6 5 4 3 2

Printed and bound in the EU.

Contents

Acknowledgements

Thanks to the following people: my wife Noreen, sons Patrick and David, and daughter Lisa. Grateful appreciation to the National Library of Ireland, Dublin; the staff of the James Hardiman Library, NUIG: Michael Faherty, Marie Boran, Liam Frehan, Michael O'Connor, Geraldine Curtain, Anne Mitchell; County Galway Library and staff at Island House: Maureen Moran and Mary Kavanagh. Thanks to Tom Small, Tom Joe Furey, Angela O'Toole, David Courtney and the late Paddy O'Neill. To all in the media: Galway Bay FM, RTÉ Raidió na Gaeltachta, *Connacht Tribune*, *The Tuam Herald*, *Galway Advertiser* and *Galway Independent*, including those who gave excellent publicity to this project; and to Declan Dooley, Hilary Martyn, Brendan Carroll, Dave Hickey, Joe O'Shaughnessy, Ronnie O'Gorman, Dickie Byrne, Éamonn Howley, Mark Kennedy, Tom Kenny, Keith Finnegan, Tom Gilmore, Jim Carney, Mary Conroy, Peadar O'Dowd, Des Kelly, Máirtin Tom Sheáinin, Richard 'Dick' O'Hanlon, William O'Hanlon, Mary MacDonnell, John Quinn, Alfie MacNamara, Seathran Powell, Padraic Walsh, Jonathan Margetts, Tommy Holahan, Martin Concannon, Daniel Callaghan and Sister de Lourdes Fahy.

Special thanks also to Anne Maria Furey, Kieran Hoare, Marita Silke, Laura Walsh, James Casserly, Bob and Mary

Waller, and Bill and Alice Scanlan for proofreading my work and making many valuable suggestions. I am again deeply indebted to a very special friend, Jacqueline O'Brien, who has, as always, given so generously of her time, researching, proofreading and giving expert advice, encouragement and support throughout this project.

Preface

The Black and Tans is a name that even today can still evoke anger and disgust in many people because of the way that group treated the Irish during their short stay here in the early 1920s. Imagine the uproar there would be today if the British government hired drunken hooligans, gave them uniforms and guns, and sent them to Ireland to fight the natives. The Black and Tans in their day were ill-disciplined thugs in uniform, paid 10 shillings a day to make Ireland a 'hell for the rebels'. *Blood for Blood* paints a vivid picture of the fearful times that the people of Galway were forced to endure under the Black and Tan regime.

The government forces in Ireland during the War of Independence were four pronged: not only had they the trained regular army and police, but they also employed the war-hardened Auxiliaries and the ill-disciplined rabble in the Black and Tans. Against them stood the rebels of Galway, who had a burning fervour to fight the last great fight for Irish freedom after 800 years of domination. And fight they did, day and night, though often badly armed and trying to hold down a job to provide some sort of income for themselves and their families.

In spite of the huge odds stacked against these rebels, and the certainty of a savage punishment or death if the Tans got their hands on them, one must ask why they fought as they did. Why for instance would Michael Walsh of the Old Malt House in High Street in Galway, a married father with eight children, who had every reason in the world to take a back seat, still play an active part in the War of Independence? The description of the Tans marching Michael Walsh through the streets of Galway before murdering him on the Long Walk is surely one of the most poignant and heart-rending stories in this book.

There is a saying in Irish '*is fearr beannacht amháin i do bheo ná dhá bheannacht déag i do bhás*' (it is better to get one blessing while you're alive than twelve blessings after you've died). Our *beannacht amháin* goes to William Henry for telling this remarkable story of the remarkable men and women of Galway who are featured in this book. 'Why?' has a straightforward answer – they were prepared to pay any sacrifice, including the ultimate one that many of them did, because of their love for Ireland. The sacrifices of these brave people deserve to be remembered and great credit is due to William Henry for the precise and vivid manner in which he tells their story.

The noble story of this fight for Irish freedom is personal even today for lots of people. My own father Pat, now in his mid-nineties, has a memory of the Tans putting a bullet through the thatched roof of his home in Tír an Fhia, Leitir Mór, while they were searching for a local activist, Joe Lee. In my own home parish of Castlegar, described by William Henry in this book as 'a hotbed of republican activity at the time', I was very familiar as a youngster with some of the rebels who were active during the War of Independence. Families throughout Galway must be particularly proud of their loved ones who took part, many of whom suffered ongoing health issues due to the hardships they suffered during the struggle. It was the last great fight for Irish freedom, at least for the twenty-six counties that now make up the Republic. Despite troubled times and all that we have presently, it is still our country. Contrast that to the Welsh and the Scots, who will roar themselves hoarse in their efforts to beat the Sassenachs in a rugby international on Saturday, and then on Monday return themselves to be governed again from London.

We humbly give the *dhá bheannacht déag* to those men and women who fearlessly waved the maroon and white, as well as the tricolour, in their fight for Ireland's freedom. As you will read in this fine book, you will see that we owe them a lot.

Joe Connolly, 2012

Introduction

One could consider many reasons for the rise of nationalism and republican ideals in late nineteenth- and early twentieth-century Ireland, but memories of the Great Famine of 1845–50 and its aftermath of evictions and poverty were certainly some of the crucial ones. The last decades of the nineteenth century saw the birth of the Land League, the Gaelic League, the Gaelic Athletic Association and other such organisations, giving people hope of gaining control over the land they worked and a pride in their Irish heritage. It also gave rise to a generation of Irish people with a strong determination to effect change, even if that meant bloodshed.

When one looks at the 1916 rebellion, Galway was one of the few places outside Dublin that came out in force in support of the rebel cause. This momentous occasion paved the way for the War of Independence, locally known as the Black and Tan War, and those who fought in the latter conflict got a second chance to fight for the same cause, although using methods very different from those employed during the Easter rebellion. The War of Independence was fought not as a pitched battle, but mainly as a guerrilla war.

The story of Galway's War of Independence has not been fully told before. Those who fought risked all against the Black and Tans and their colleagues, the Auxiliaries, who were ruthless in their attempts to defeat the IRA and used every means to do so, including murder. In the writing of this book I have used excerpts from the witness statements of those Irish men and women who fought this brutal campaign, as well as contemporary newspaper accounts from those critical years. I also interviewed family members of those who fought and checked many local histories and documents to ensure that all avenues of research were covered in my recording of this important period of history.

Blood for Blood opens with the Galway Volunteers marching out in 1916 to make their stand for Ireland. The story unfolds chronologically, and the reader can see the terrifying situation develop and deteriorate into mayhem and murder, where even pregnant mothers and priests were attacked. I also look at the isolation of, and dangerous situations experienced by, members of the domestic police force, the Royal Irish Constabulary (RIC), as barracks after barracks was attacked. The arrival of the Black and Tans to reinforce policing numbers led to a huge upsurge in violence. As this force began its campaign to control the streets, almost the entire population lived in terror as its members exploited their power, seeking out victims, raiding and plundering.

Ambush was the main method used by the IRA to fight back against the RIC and Tans. However, this brought about even more fear among the general public as the Tans and Auxiliaries sought revenge through bloody reprisals. September 1920 saw a real escalation of violence in Galway, which continued without mercy until the signing of the Truce, almost a year later. During this period many local people were killed, some in the streets, others shot in their homes. A legacy of hate developed, which has left bitter memories.

Outlying towns and villages were not spared either: Oranmore, Tuam, Ardrahan, Headford and Clifden felt the full impact of Tan and Auxiliary violence. These areas came under brutal attack and many homes and businesses were burned and destroyed. People were forced to flee their homes, in many cases without their belongings, leaving them almost destitute.

This book also tells the story of those Galway people singled out for murder in rural and urban areas. It was a time of little trust in strangers; suspicion was part of everyday life. The intelligence network of the IRA is examined and examples of how informers were caught and severely dealt with are described.

William Henry

1

Rebellion in Galway

Just over a week before the 1916 Easter Rising, Liam Mellows arrived back in Ireland. Mellows had been born in 1892 in Lancashire, where his father, a British soldier, was stationed. The family moved to Dublin while Mellows was still a child. As a young man, he became involved in a number of Irish nationalist organisations and in 1913 he joined the Irish Republican Brotherhood (IRB), a secretive republican organisation that was determined to gain independence from British rule using any means necessary. Mellows was also involved in the Irish Volunteers, which was set up in November 1913 as a paramilitary nationalist force originally formed to reinforce the Irish demand for Home Rule. The following year Mellows was sent to south Galway to take command of and organise the Volunteers there.

In March 1916 Mellows was arrested in Athenry and was imprisoned in Arbour Hill Barracks while awaiting deportation to England. The authorities arranged to have Mellows placed with relatives in Leek, Staffordshire. However, he was vital to the Galway rebellion, and so the IRB, with the help of his mother who visited him regularly, made sure they were aware of his location at all times. Despite the fact that his movements were seriously restricted and he was kept under constant surveillance, a plan involving his brother, Barney, who bore a striking resemblance to him, was devised to free Mellows. When Barney Mellows reached the house where his brother was staying, both men retired to one of the bedrooms, where they immediately switched clothes and Liam left in the guise of his brother. In the pocket of the coat, Mellows found a sailing ticket for Ireland, plus detailed instructions on what to do upon arrival in Dublin.

Shortly after arriving in the capital, Mellows went to the home of the Pearse family where he was to stay. By the end of Holy Week he had returned to County Galway and set about finalising the plans for the rebellion due to take place on Easter Sunday. During that week the Galway Volunteer officers called a meeting to discuss their role in the coming rebellion. These men included Éamonn Corbett, Michael Joseph Howley (always known as Joe), Padraic Fahy, Matthew Neilan and their commanding officer, Larry Lardner from Athenry. It was decided at this meeting that Lardner would travel to Dublin to clarify instructions for the rebellion. Unfortunately, when he arrived in the capital he could not locate Patrick Pearse or Eoin MacNeill, leader of the Irish Volunteers. He did meet Bulmer Hobson, who instructed him not to obey any orders unless they were signed by MacNeill. Lardner returned to Galway with these orders.

Meanwhile, Éamonn Ceannt had sent a dispatch to

Lardner with instructions for the planned rebellion. The messenger was unable to locate Lardner and instead gave the orders to Éamonn Corbett: 'Collect the Premiums 7 p.m. Sunday – P. H. Pearse'.[1] This was the agreed code to signal that the rebellion would go ahead. However, the following day Lardner received orders from MacNeill suspending manoeuvres. An emergency meeting was held at the home of prominent nationalist George Nicholas in Galway city. Although Mellows was not mentioned as having attended this meeting, it was likely he was there given his rank as senior officer. It was decided to proceed with preparations for action while sending another messenger to Dublin to clarify the conflicting orders. This messenger was unsuccessful in doing so.

On Easter Sunday, after learning of the sinking of the *Aud*, which was carrying arms to be used in the rebellion, MacNeill published orders in the *Sunday Independent* calling off all Volunteer action on that day. Mellows learned of the orders and reluctantly prepared to cancel the rebellion. The following day Volunteers in Athenry received a dispatch from Dublin: 'We are out from twelve o'clock today. Issue your orders without delay. – P.H.P.'[2] There was still some doubt and uncertainty among the men, but later that afternoon the Dublin train brought news of the outbreak of rebellion in the capital. Dispatches were immediately issued to the South Galway Volunteers and about 500 badly armed men joined the rebellion.

In Oranmore Volunteers under the command of Captain

Joe Howley began placing explosives under the bridge leading into the village and the RIC evacuated the barracks there. On the arrival of British troops and police reinforcements from Renmore Barracks and Galway city, shots were exchanged and the rebels were forced to withdraw. Mellows, who had by this point arrived at Oranmore, provided covering fire for Joe Howley and his men, and during the retreat several policemen were wounded. According to the Galway correspondent for the *Connacht Tribune*, these Volunteers actually came within three miles of the city on Tuesday, but had to retreat because of shellfire from naval gun ships in Galway Bay.[3]

In Castlegar the Volunteers had also mobilised, under Captain Brian Molloy. Other senior members of the Castlegar unit included Michael Newell and Tom Ruane. The plan was to link up with the Claregalway Company, then to go to Lydican, Loughgeorge and Kilcon and force the police to surrender. In preparation for the rebellion, Michael Newell, a blacksmith, had been manufacturing pike heads during the weeks leading up to the Rising and just a week before the rebellion he was almost arrested when police arrived at his forge. He managed to hide the incriminating evidence, but was warned that he would be charged under the Defence of the Realm Act if caught with weapons of any kind. Nevertheless, he resumed his work with such vigour that he was in a position to supply pike heads to the Spiddal company as well as his own.

On Easter Monday the Castlegar Company collected additional shotguns from farmers around the district. At about 4 p.m. on Tuesday, Brian Molloy received orders from Mellows to mobilise, as the Rising was already under way. The Castlegar men reacted immediately and marched to Carnmore crossroads to link up with the Claregalway Company. The men then went towards Oranmore to join forces with the main Volunteer army. On the way they received information that Mellows and his men had moved to Athenry. Rather than have all the men march there, Molloy sent Lieutenant Thomas Newell (always known as Sweeney), a brother of Michael, to Athenry to make contact with Mellows and await new orders. Molloy meanwhile returned to Carnmore and billeted his men in local farmhouses and barns.

The next afternoon Molloy received instructions to march to link up with the Volunteers from Athenry. As they proceeded, Michael Newell noticed a girl on a hill in the distance waving a white apron. The girl was Sheila (Bina) King, and she was trying to warn the men of impending danger – a large force of police, a convoy of thirteen cars, was heading in their direction. Molloy ordered his men to take cover behind some field boundary walls and then, as the police were within striking distance, the rebels opened fire.

The police convoy halted about 100 yards from the rebel position. There were possibly six policemen to each car and they began advancing towards the Volunteers, firing as they went. The fire was intense and bullets continuously clipped the top of the wall, so the Volunteers found it difficult to return fire. When the police reached the crossroads, they stopped, and Constable P. Whelan shouted at the Volunteers to surrender, saying that he knew who they were. He was immediately shot dead and the police inspector, who was just behind him, was wounded. The police reacted by trying to outflank the rebels, but were beaten back and more men were wounded. They then rushed back to their vehicles and drove off in the direction of Oranmore.

Once the immediate danger had passed, Molloy ordered his men to fall in and they continued their march to rebel headquarters, which had been set up in the agricultural college and model farm near Athenry. As they came close to their destination, they again had to take cover from a large force of police who were firing at the college from the railway bridge. This attack was beaten off and the Castlegar and Claregalway companies entered the rebel stronghold, which was under the command of Larry Lardner. In Athenry itself, the police were virtual prisoners in their barracks. Mellows' force at this point was made up of about 500 men representing many areas, including Oranmore, Maree, Clarenbridge, Craughwell, Castlegar, Claregalway, Cregmore and Derrydonnell. Their munitions consisted of 25 rifles, 350 shotguns and an assortment of small arms.

Although most of the country was against the rebellion, this does not seem to have been the case in the rebel-held areas of south Galway, where the local population welcomed those taking part. The absence of landlords, land agents and armed police, who were afraid to venture into areas of rebel activity, had given the locals their first glimpse of a free society. Farmers' wives and daughters supplied the Volunteers with freshly baked bread, washed down with milk, and some were given meals in farmhouses.

On Wednesday evening the Volunteers at Athenry moved to Moyode Castle, the unoccupied home of the Persse family, and Mellows made it his headquarters. By now British troops and marines had landed at Galway docks and were preparing for action against the rebels. Several Volunteer officers in Galway city, among them George Nicholas, were arrested and taken on board one of the warships.

At Moyode animals were slaughtered as required and the women of the Republican women's paramilitary organisation, Cumann na mBan, acted as cooks. In the distance, the sound of naval artillery fire could be heard coming from the direction of Galway Bay. On Thursday evening the Volunteers held a meeting and it was decided to disband the unarmed men, thus reducing the force to about 400. Although he had not seen any real action, Mellows said that he was determined to fight to the last man if necessary. However, when they became aware that police from the northern counties were now arriving in County Galway and arresting Volunteers who were making their way home, the majority of his officers argued in favour of disbanding.

On Friday evening the remainder of the Volunteers, about 150, moved south until they reached a large and unoccupied mansion at Limepark and set up another headquarters. A local priest, Fr Thomas Fahy, brought news that British troops were on the move from Athlone and Ballinasloe, sweeping the countryside towards Galway. He also informed them that the rebellion in Dublin was collapsing. After hearing this news, Mellows reluctantly disbanded the Volunteers. Most returned to their homes, but three of the men, Frank Hynes, Peadar Howley and Ailbhe Ó Monacháin (Alf Monahan), chose to remain with Mellows and became fugitives with him. Having taken shelter in a number of locations in the mountains and wooded areas, they eventually found a safe refuge at Tulla, just south of Kinvara.

Mellows remained there for four months, during which time he visited Kinvara, where he took shelter in the Convent of Mercy of St Joseph. The authorities were obviously informed of the visit, because they conducted a search. When Fr Thomas Burke, the local parish priest, was informed of these actions, he was outraged and wrote a letter of protest to General Sir John Maxwell, the senior British officer in Dublin. In his reply, Maxwell stated that the local police sergeant had been informed through an anonymous letter that Mellows was hiding in the convent. He went on to say that the sergeant felt it was his duty to capture Mellows and that, as far as he was concerned, the search was 'carried out with perfect decorum'. After evading capture for a number of months, Mellows made his way to Liverpool, and from there managed to secure a passage on board a steamer bound for America.

Following the surrender, Captain Brian Molloy and Michael Newell also went on the run, but were later captured. Molloy was sentenced to ten years' penal servitude for his part in the Rising; however, he was released in June 1917. A short time later, he was back in charge of the Castlegar Company, with Sweeney Newell as his first lieutenant. Michael Newell was sent to Frongoch and was later transferred to Wormwood Scrubs. He appeared before the Sankey Commission and was questioned regarding his movements on the day Constable Whelan was shot dead. He was then informed that smoke had been seen coming out of his rifle. He admitted being there that day, but stated that he was armed with a shotgun. Following the inquiry Newell was returned to Frongoch and was released on Christmas Eve 1916.

Most of the men involved in the Easter rebellion continued their involvement in the Volunteers and would go on to play their part in the War of Independence. In preparation for renewed hostilities, Seamus Murphy, a senior Irish Volunteer activist from Dublin, arrived in Galway during the spring of 1918 to form the Galway Brigade and begin serious military training. He acted as the brigade's officer commanding (OC) and used the grounds of Ballybrit racecourse to put his men through their paces. By the start of 1919 their presence there was becoming well known throughout Galway and as an act of defiance the Volunteers mounted tricolour flags on all the poles in the racecourse grounds the night before the Galway races later that year. This grabbed the attention of the thousands of people arriving for the race meeting and gave the police additional duties to perform that day, as the flags had to be taken down.

While the training was going well, the Volunteers were still badly equipped for the inevitable clash with British forces, so they began raiding the houses of local gentry in a bid to secure arms. Information gathering about the enemy was also critical and members of the Castlegar unit, including Michael and Sweeney Newell and Joseph Donnellan, were ordered to hold up mail cars on their way from Galway and seize any British mail. This was successful and, as much of the information gathering was done by Michael Newell, he was appointed battalion intelligence officer.[4]

In late January 1919 two events occurred which would mark the start of the renewed fight for independence in Ireland.

2

Apostles of Freedom

By the start of 1919 it had become clear that the British government was not going to revisit its promise of introducing Home Rule to Ireland. Despite the passing of the Third Home Rule Bill in 1914, its implementation was put off when war broke out and it was never revived. Ireland was also excluded from the Paris Peace Conference, the meeting of the Allied victors after the First World War, which was to outline peace terms for the defeated countries and redraw the map of Europe with new borders and countries. Despite an estimated 49,400 Irishmen giving their lives for a fight that they had been told was in the cause of the freedom of small nations, Ireland herself seemed to have gained little.[1]

In response, on 21 January 1919, Ireland's first Dáil Éireann convened in the Mansion House in Dublin and unanimously adopted the Declaration of Irish Independence. Meanwhile, in a little place called Soloheadbeg in County Tipperary, members of the Third Tipperary Brigade of the Irish Volunteers embarked on a more violent start to the campaign to secure Irish independence. On that same day a group of men from the Third Tipperary, led by Seán Treacy, Dan Breen and Seamus Robinson, planned to seize a cartload of explosives destined for a nearby quarry. The two men transporting the explosives were being escorted by two members of the RIC, Constables James McDonnell and Patrick O'Connell. When the group was ambushed by the republicans, the two policemen were shot dead. These were the first shots fired at British forces in Ireland since 1916 and they were also the first shots of the War of Independence.[2]

The violence quickly spread throughout the country and it was obvious that Galway would be seriously affected, considering that over 500 men had turned out for the rebellion in 1916. Most of these men had been interned in Britain alongside others from all over the country. The British had in a sense contributed to their own demise in Ireland, not simply by arresting a large number of innocent men, but also by placing Volunteers from various regions in the same prison camps, thus introducing them to each other. Contact details were exchanged and, once they were released, a more organised Volunteer movement emerged.

The war that these men embarked upon in 1919 was totally different from the 1916 rebellion: it would be fought using guerrilla tactics. These proved remarkably effective and the British military was forced to intensify its efforts in an attempt to root out the rebels. From January 1919 to March 1920 there were over 20,000 military raids on houses throughout the country, resulting in almost 400 arrests. Proclamations were also introduced to suppress meetings and gatherings.

Despite this, republican attacks became more frequent, while in Dublin, Michael Collins, who had been appointed minister for finance in the Dáil, was organising a centralised intelligence system which would provide a vital resource in the fight against the British.[3]

While the Irish had failed to gain representation at the Paris Peace Conference, there were many delegates attending who had a serious interest in Irish affairs. In May 1919 the American envoys to the Paris Peace Conference visited Galway. They were referred to by the media as 'Apostles of Freedom'. The Commissioners, Michael Ryan and Frank Walsh, and the Governor of Illinois, Edward Dunne, arrived by train. The *Galway Express* gave a detailed and colourful description of their visit. The train had stopped at each station on its journey to Galway, where the envoys had taken the time to address the crowds. Michael Ryan spoke at Athenry, telling the people to continue the glorious fight and urging them to be firm in their beliefs, saying that millions of people were behind them now, more so than ever before in Irish history. He told them not to expect too much too soon, but ultimate victory was certain – Ireland would be a nation and a Republic. There was an overwhelming response when he finished speaking.

When the party arrived in Galway the cheers and applause drowned out the sound of the welcoming St Patrick's Band assembled in the station. There was a distinguished gathering on the platform of leading clergy, university men, local and national politicians and republican leaders. These included Dáil Éireann and cabinet ministers William Cosgrave,

Richard Mulcahy, Eoin MacNeill and many more. The area in front of the Railway Hotel at Eyre Square was cordoned off by members of the Irish Volunteers, who also formed a guard of honour. The president of the Galway branch of Sinn Féin, L. E. O'Dea, extended a warm welcome to the visitors on behalf of the people. When he had finished speaking, Michael Ryan was invited to take the stand. He thanked the people of Galway for such an enormous reception and said that since the train had crossed the Shannon every Connacht hill had been alive with huge fires of welcome. These, he said, were a symbol of the old fires of freedom, fires of victory which had now been relit. There was an immediate response from the crowd of cheering and applause, which stopped him momentarily from speaking.

When the crowd fell silent, Ryan reminded them that there were over twenty million of their 'kindred' who found homes in the 'Great Republic to the West' – this set the crowd off again. When he had regained their attention, he evoked the principles of the Great War, saying, 'This was a people's war, a war waged not for conquest, not for trade, not for vengeance, but in order that the blessings and principles of democracy might be extended to all the peoples of the world.' Before the crowd could react, Ryan called out that thousands of Irishmen had laid down their lives in the belief that the promise of freedom would be honoured once the war had ended. 'These men were lied to,' he shouted. 'Ireland was not even considered when all the countries of Europe were sitting at the table of freedom in Paris.' Speaking of the Irish in the

United States, he said that their hearts were saddened that the people of Ireland had the chalice of liberty at her lips, yet she was denied the 'drink of freedom'. He continued, 'Your oppressor had the ears of the world, and you were muzzled … Fellow-men this Irish cause of yours is to the forefront of the world's conflict.'

Ryan then told those gathered that 5,132 delegates had recently met in the city of Philadelphia and adopted a motion put forward by the leader of the Catholic Church in America supporting the Irish people's age-old struggle for liberty. Jews, Methodists, those who worshipped at many different altars, also endorsed this motion. He reminded them of the suffering of the Irish people during the famine, incorrectly quoting the supposed comment of *The Times* of London about the demise of the Irish: 'Thank God the Celts are going.' (No such comment appeared in *The Times* during the famine.) He also reminded the crowd that Irishmen had been fighting against oppression in Connacht for centuries and thousands had died because of English tyranny. He said that God would never have allowed the Irish people to endure the scaffold, dungeon, exile and famine, 'if He did not mean to give to some generation of our race the dazzling vision of Ireland a Nation'. Ryan ended by saying that the day of glory – the cause for which soldiers had died, poets had sung and people had prayed – was coming, 'the day was close when Ireland would be a Nation once again'.

Fr O'Flanagan, one of the organising committee, was then introduced to the crowd. He began, 'Fellow citizens of the

Irish Republic …', but before he could continue the crowd erupted with cheers of support on hearing these words. When the applauding and shouting had died down, he welcomed the envoys from the United States, whom he said were representing some twenty million Irish-Americans. He went on to speak about how America had entered the Great War in support of the freedom of small nations, not to prop up empires. Lies, he said, were perpetrated on the small countries of Europe to draw them into a struggle between two empires, and it was time now to right the wrongs. The problem now faced, O'Flanagan continued, had arisen because some Irish people had allowed themselves to fall away from the ideals of a free Irish nation: 'The talk about Home Rule, Repeal of the Union, the Colonial Home Rule, and such other mockeries of national liberty, blinded us from the real dazzling vision of a free and independent Ireland … The great opportunity that came to us with the big European war went by, and the Irish people did not awaken sufficiently to seize the opportunity.' He reminded those gathered of past generations who had to fight in darker days and said that there was much pride in the fact that the west was now awake, Ireland was awake and the flag of Ireland was nailed to the mast, and that the Irish were free in soul if not in body. He said that he truly believed that it would not be very long before the Irish Republican flag would fly without rival from one end of the country to the other. These comments were met with a huge response of cheering and continued applause.

On Sunday a large reception was held in the Town Hall

in honour of the delegates. The building was decorated with Republican flags and photographs of the executed leaders of the 1916 rebellion were displayed throughout. L. E. O'Dea again welcomed and thanked the American envoys for their support. He said that there was really no need to talk about the sad history of Ireland, or the terrible tyranny, as there were always brave Irishmen who fought unceasingly for their country. He insisted that Ireland should be allowed to determine its own form of government and Republic. The American delegates, he added, came to Ireland with a message of hope and support from the exiled Irish people. The message was clear: if their old nation of Ireland was deprived of its own government, then Irish-Americans would not hear of peace, except one that provided for the freedom of Ireland. The secretary of Galway Urban Council, T. Redington, then read an address from the people of Galway, which reiterated almost everything that the other speakers had said. When he finished, Edward Dunne, on behalf of the American delegates, addressed the gathering and thanked them for the fantastic welcome they had received since arriving in Galway and indeed Ireland. During his speech, he pledged continued support for the Irish cause. He spoke about his mother being from Galway and how, when he was growing up, she always told him of 'this great city'.

There were other meetings held and speeches made over the next few days, all promoting a free, independent Ireland, a land in control of its own destiny. The American visitors were described as 'Apostles of Freedom' and their visit was a serious endorsement of the fight for Irish freedom. Given the rousing speeches, the harassment by the military and the British government's failure to implement the promises made to so many Irishmen who had fought in the Great War, it was inevitable that attacks against the British and thus reprisals would intensify.[4]

3

Isolation and Danger

While raids on houses produced some arms, if the war was to continue the IRA would have to build up a large supply of weapons, which meant that it would have to become more daring. (The Volunteers became commonly known as the IRA during 1919 after the formation of the Dáil.) It became crucial to extend raids to police stations in order to increase fire power.

One of the first of these attacks took place on 25 May 1919 at Loughgeorge, a village some nine miles from Galway city. A combined force from the Galway city and Castlegar units made their way to Loughgeorge in the early hours of the morning. Some of them took up positions on the outskirts of the village to warn of any enemy reinforcements that might attempt to relieve the barracks.[1] Seán Broderick from Prospect Hill was the acting IRA OC.[2] Born on 8 February 1900, Broderick was a carpenter by trade and worked in MacDonagh and Sons in Merchants Road.[3] He had joined the Volunteers in 1917 and quickly rose through the ranks. Broderick seems to have had a natural military ability, training various companies and securing arms and ammunition from British soldiers, by purchase or 'otherwise'.[4]

Another Volunteer who took part in this attack was Jim Furey from Oranmore, who had joined the Volunteers in 1917 and by 1920 was heavily involved in republican activities with the Castlegar company. He was courting Gretta Newell, a sister of the two republican brothers. Gretta was an excellent Irish dancer and gave performances around the county to raise funds for the IRA's coffers. It was during this time that she met Furey.

The barracks at Loughgeorge was occupied by about twelve policemen on the night of the attack. Despite the roof being set on fire and a sustained gun battle, the garrison refused to surrender. By morning the attack had to be aborted as the alarm had been raised and it was only a matter of time before police reinforcements arrived. Although the attack itself failed, it was successful in the sense that it had shown the authorities just how vulnerable their outlying positions could be, so far from reinforcements in Galway city.[5]

The police in Galway responded by coming out in force to disrupt Sinn Féin meetings. In October 1919 one such meeting in Ballinasloe was baton-charged by police, who were also armed with rifles and hand grenades. The attack was described as brutal and savage, and the day was a sad one for many people, as Irishman attacked Irishman in the name of a foreign government. Some of these men knew each other, which made the situation even worse and caused long-term resentment between them. There was also much bitterness caused by the fact that many of the men who were attacked had served in Europe.[6]

In many areas, the police stopped innocent people, who were simply going about their daily routine, for questioning, although in some cases they clearly had cause for suspicion. In September 1919, near Kilkerrin, Connemara, a man named Michael Kelly was stopped on his motorbike by the police because he had registration plates painted in the colours of the Irish Republic. He was taken to court because the plates did not comply with the local government regulations. The man was fined, told to remove the colours and had to pay costs.[7] It was obviously decided that while he was advertising his politics, he posed no real danger. It was the people who did not so prominently display their political views who would prove the most dangerous.

The raids, road blocks and stopping of people in the streets continued, but by January 1920 the situation for the British forces was deteriorating across the country. On 20 January, Constable Luke Finnegan from Dunmore, County Galway, was shot and mortally wounded outside his house in Thurles. He was a married man with two children. It was unclear why he was singled out. He had only just finished duty and was on his way home. His wife told the police that she was upstairs in her room when she heard three gunshots. She ran and opened the window and, looking out, saw her husband staggering. He looked at her and said, 'Mary, I am done, what will you and the little babies do?'

The police and medics arrived and took Finnegan to

Steven's Hospital in Dublin, but it was too late – he died a short time later.[8]

Immediately after the attack, orders were issued to all policemen to report for duty. A battalion of Sherwood Foresters joined forces with the police and attacked several buildings in Thurles with hand grenades and fired shots into the business premises of known Sinn Féin members. The office of the *Tipperary Star* newspaper was also attacked. The people living in Thurles were subjected to complete terror for over two hours, with gunfire and explosions being heard throughout the town.[9]

Another Galway constable, twenty-two-year-old John Heanue from Tullycross, near Clifden, was killed in County Tipperary some weeks later. He had just finished a patrol in the village of Ragg with a colleague, Constable Michael Flaherty, and the men called into a public house and grocer's shop owned by Laurence Fanning. They noticed three men sitting at the other end of the bar who shouted 'Hands up!' and drew revolvers. Heanue immediately leapt over the counter and, drawing his weapon, began firing on the assailants. The men returned fire, mortally wounding him, and then ran from the premises. Constable Flaherty followed and fired after them, but they were soon out of sight. The remains of John Heanue were returned to Clifden the following day for burial.[10]

Attacks on police barracks became more common as time progressed. In early January 1920 the IRA attacked the police station in Castlehacket, in the north of the county. They first cut the telephone wires and set up barricades on approach roads to the barracks. One of the policemen on duty that night heard a noise outside. As he walked towards the window to investigate, it was shattered by a bullet and some of the glass fragments lodged in his face. This was followed by continuous gunfire, taking the police by surprise. Some of the windows were protected by sandbags, which helped the police considerably, as the attackers were forced to climb nearby trees to try to find a target. In doing so, they became targets themselves. The attack lasted about two hours, during which time the police reported that they had fired some 300 shots. The attack was called off when a police patrol, on hearing the shooting, came to the aid of their comrades. There were no serious casualties, but the barracks was severely damaged.[11]

The police barracks at Barna, just west of Galway city, and Killeen, in the east of the county, were also attacked that same month, causing the police to evacuate these positions.[12] Over the following months many more police stations were to find themselves in the same position of isolation and danger. Kiltormer Barracks near Ballinasloe was forced to close in February.[13]

On the night of 22 March a well-organised IRA attack was carried out on Castlegrove Barracks, near Dunmore. The police were isolated for a time as the telegraph wires had been cut. The attack began with an explosion at one of the gables of the barracks. The bomb split the gable and the chimney collapsed as a barrage of gunfire was opened up on the building. There were nine heavily armed policemen on duty and fire was returned immediately through the broken windows. The gunfight went on for almost three hours, but there were no casualties. At about 5 a.m. a whistle sounded, the signal for the rebels to retire. Somehow news of the attack had reached the military in Galway and they had left the town in force to come to the aid of their beleaguered colleagues. The convoy included motor cars, army lorries and armoured vehicles. When it reached Merlin Park, it was forced off the road, as local units of the IRA had cut down trees across the route in preparation for the arrival of back-up.[14] The convoy drove through the fields for a short distance and picked up the road further on. Approaching Clarenbridge, it came across similar obstacles. This time the convoy was held up even longer, and thus prevented from reaching Castlegrove Barracks. However, other police barracks along the route were reinforced. As a result of this attack, Castlegrove Barracks was largely destroyed and the garrison was evacuated to Tuam.

In April, Abbeyknockmoy (near Tuam) and Monivea (just north-east of Galway city) Barracks were both destroyed by explosives. In the same month the station in Barnaderg, ten miles from Tuam, was raided. The only occupants at the time were the wife of Sergeant Cain and her children. They were taken to safety by the IRA before the barracks was blown up.[15] The police barracks in Moycullen and Inverin suffered a similar fate that same month.[16]

On 1 July 1920 the Brookeen RIC Barracks, located about midway between Loughrea and Athenry, was attacked by a large party of IRA. It was defended by seven policemen and the gun-battle went on for over two hours. Bombs were also used in the attack, causing much damage to the building. Military reinforcements were again held up by barricades erected along the route. The police had to fight their way out of the station with automatic gunfire and hand grenades after the roof was set alight. By the time the military arrived, the barracks was completely destroyed. The police estimated that about 200 men took part in the attack, and while such estimates were usually exaggerated, it still unnerved the authorities.[17]

During that same week Tyrone House near Ballinderreen was burned to the ground. The house was the former home of the St George family, but, with the exception of a caretaker, had been unoccupied for some years.[18] It seems that the caretaker was ill at the time and was taken to safety before the house was set alight. The following night the Gurtymadden Barracks, near Loughrea, was attacked and destroyed; this was followed by the evacuation of Ferbane Barracks near Woodford, County Galway, which was then burned by the IRA.[19]

That same month Kinvara Barracks was evacuated and the departure of the police was heralded by a series of explosions set off by the IRA in an attempt to seal off the town. They surrounded the area and upon entering the town proceeded to demolish the barracks, leaving only one wall standing, from which they hung the tricolour. They then marched to the courthouse, singing the 'Soldiers' Song', where they removed all the public records and law books and set them alight in the middle of the street.[20]

One by one police forces in small, rural villages abandoned their posts or were forced out by attacks. On 14 July 1920 the police garrison was evacuated from the Aran Islands and arrived in Galway on a trawler fitted with arms. Even the barracks in Salthill was deserted.[21] By mid July the local authorities announced that the main police stations which remained open were Galway, Tuam, Oughterard and Headford.[22] Although attacked several times, Portumna Barracks also managed to survive. By the end of July, Caltra, Williamstown, Cummer, Woodford and many more barracks had closed. The barracks at the docks in Galway had also closed earlier in the year, but the Galway Harbour Commissioners protested about its closure and it was reopened after a short time.[23]

The military decided to put on a show of strength at Portumna and on 15 July troops from the Scot Greys and Royal Dragoons arrived in the town in army trucks. They were accompanied by armoured cars and were equipped with Lewis machine guns, twenty-pounder guns and various other weapons. They set up road blocks and no one was allowed through without being searched. This continued for several days before the soldiers were ordered to return to Ballinasloe.[24]

The evacuated police from a number of barracks were stationed temporarily in Dominick Street and Eglinton Street, Galway. Some of the policemen were feeling the pressure, as in large towns they knew that they probably lived in close proximity to members of the republican movement, but in many cases were unaware of the identity of these people. This made policemen somewhat nervous as they went about their daily routines. Resentment from the local population also caused much anxiety, resulting in six policemen at Dominick

Street tendering their resignations. Upon hearing the news, Inspector Routledge – one of the head constables – went to speak with the men. He gave them startling news, saying that the RIC was going to be disbanded within six months and a new force would be formed. He warned them that they would lose their gratuities by resigning now and it would be more beneficial for them to remain in the force until the new organisation was in place. After some discussion, they decided to remain, at least for the remainder of the year, and await any new developments.[25]

Sergeant Donegan of the Dominick Street Barracks later denied that any of his men had threatened to resign. He stated that the 'wholesale' evacuation of police stations was really a reorganisation measure taken by the force because the men did not wish to spend the winter in isolated areas. Donegan also said that there was no danger for the future of the RIC and denied any knowledge of the force being disbanded.[26]

There were, however, large numbers of police resigning throughout the country. In August 1920 the RIC authorities themselves announced that between 1 May and 31 July there were some 556 resignations from the force, but they were quick to add that new recruits numbered 816 that year.[27] Nevertheless, the republicans were forcing the police back into the population centres, where the situation would only deteriorate.

4

Terrorising the Terrorists

Ambushes and house raids by the IRA in Galway also became more daring during 1920. The first ambush that year took place in January, when a party of military officers from Renmore Barracks was attacked near Moyvilla, Athenry. The officers were on their way to a ball being hosted by the Persse family in Roxboro House. The car in which the soldiers were travelling was hit several times, but the military managed to return fire immediately. A sharp gunfight ensued, which ended when the attackers withdrew. A number of other cars were also fired on that night – all were on their way to Roxboro.[1]

Mail cars were also being targeted and letters taken in an attempt to intercept those addressed to the police. A post box located in a wall in Knockcarra was removed and taken away by republicans. Such actions were of grave concern to the authorities, as much of the information that they received from other police personnel – orders, information and so on – came through the mail. An additional worry was that informers sometimes used the post to ensure their information reached the police without the risk of being seen entering a police station.[2]

In February 1920 the IRA raided the home of Lord Killanin's chauffeur in Spiddal and searched the house for arms. They came away empty-handed as the man was unarmed and they did not gain access to the main house. It was reported that because of this attack Lord Killanin left Spiddal and moved to his residence in London.[3] A few nights later, a former British soldier named Patrick Thornton from Loughanbeg, Spiddal, was shot dead near his home. The attack was believed to have been carried out by republicans.[4] Carrack Lodge in Clonbur, the home of Captain Barrett, a British officer living in the area, was also raided by an armed and masked gang and some guns were taken.[5]

On 15 February an attempt was made to blow up the home of Captain Henry Dudley Hodgeson near Oughterard. A hole was dug at the gable of the house and fourteen pieces of gelignite were packed into a box, which was then placed in the hole and covered with mud. A fuse was attached to the bomb, but it failed to detonate, part of it being defective. Had it exploded, it would have caused serious damage and possibly loss of life. Three local men were arrested and were taken to Galway Jail to await trial.[6]

In May the home of Francis Persse in Cloonmore, Roscahill, was targeted, when a party of armed men forced their way through the front door. Several shots were fired and a number of paintings were destroyed. Persse was ordered to leave the area by the following day. People who worked for him on the estate were also targeted that night and shots were fired into the thatched roofs of their homes. These people were also

warned not to work for the Persse family again. The following morning, Persse and his wife made their way to Galway.
They were forced to leave behind most of their belongings, as
people were afraid to help them.[7]

The following month John Blake of Brooklawn House near
Tuam was shot and wounded by two men while going to mass.
He crawled to a stile in a field boundary wall where he was
found by people who had come to investigate the shooting.
They helped him to a nearby house where they secured a pony
and trap and took him home, where he was later attended by
a doctor. He had been under police protection for some time
over a land dispute, but his guard was not with him on the
morning of the attack.[8]

While many attacks and raids on manor houses were authorised by the IRA leadership, there were certain individuals
who took advantage of the situation and the vulnerability of
people. Many of these were not members of the IRA, but were
unwilling to miss out on an opportunity for personal gain in
land. One such case occurred at Castle Ellen near Athenry,
where a Captain Lambert was resident. The Lambert family
had an excellent relationship with people living in the area and
had provided secure employment over many years. Captain
Lambert was a former Connaught Ranger with an admirable
war record. Like to his father before him, he was on excellent
terms with the local people and even provided land for them
which he was not farming himself.

During the last week of January 1920 five men from the
locality approached him in the name of the Irish Republic

and demanded land from him. He refused on the grounds that he had already handed over much of his land and had little left to give. They replied by telling him that they would forcibly take the remainder of his land and plough it up to the hall door. They then threatened the men working for Lambert and warned them to cease work immediately or face the consequences. These men also received threatening letters and as a result stayed away from work. One of the men who had been threatened decided to show the letter to a member of the Sinn Féin movement living in Athenry. He then took it to his republican colleagues and, after reading the letter, the IRA stated that it had nothing to do with the threats and none of its men were involved. The IRA was angered by what had happened and, worse, that the threats had been perpetrated in the IRA's name. Members immediately went in search of the individuals responsible and warned them that if the men were not allowed back to work by the following day there would be serious consequences. The IRA also warned the culprits that if any 'evil should befall Captain Lambert' or his men at any time, the situation would be speedily taken care of and in such a manner that it would never happen again. The reporter who covered the case was delighted with the action taken by the republicans and when writing up an account of the story entitled it 'Terrorising the Terrorists'.[9]

On 4 February 1920 a similar but more serious incident took place in the village of Ardskeamore, near Corofin, about ten miles on the Galway side of Tuam. However, the target was not a manor house, but rather a thatched cottage belonging to the Lardner family. A man named Martin Cullinane from Bullaun was visiting the family that night. At about 9.30 p.m. there was a loud knock on the door. Mr Lardner opened it to six armed and masked men, who said that they were looking for arms. Lardner told them that he had no guns in the house, but the men forced their way onto the premises. Two of them remained in the kitchen with the family and their visitor, while three others began searching the house. The sixth man was armed with a shotgun and remained by the door, seeming somewhat nervous and agitated. From time to time he would hit the door, until one of the other raiders told him to stop. Martin Cullinane was standing in front of the fire facing the door when suddenly there was a gunshot and he fell, mortally wounded. Nineteen-year-old John Lardner, son of the owner, was sitting close to Cullinane and was also hit by the shotgun discharge. It was the man standing by the door who had fired the weapon, after which the raiders quickly left the house and disappeared into the night.

The following Sunday Archbishop Gilmartin of Tuam castigated and denounced the killers of Martin Cullinane. No one could understand why this pleasant-mannered man had been shot. The Archbishop described him as a respectable, inoffensive person and a good father and husband, who left a young wife and four children behind. He hoped, he added, that the 'wretch' who fired the shot had done so by accident as there was absolutely no reason for this brutal murder. The archbishop also reminded the congregation of another man who had been murdered under similar circumstances some twenty miles from Tuam just a few days earlier. This murder, he said, had been committed over land, but as Martin Cullinane was only a small farmer this could not be so in his case. The murder of Martin Cullinane was not understood, but was believed to have been over some unexplained grievance.[10]

Such incidents left many unanswered questions and some fear. Who carried out these attacks: the IRA, or individuals taking advantage of a worsening situation to settle old scores? Given the reaction by the IRA in Athenry after the Castle Ellen incident, it seems highly unlikely that these raiders were true republicans. The following incident would also point towards criminals taking advantage of the troubles now spreading across the country.

In March 1920 the parish priest of Spiddal, Fr T. MacAlinney, was held up at gunpoint by a small group of masked men while returning from a funeral. They forced him to hand over his money and then made off into the darkness. Many local people felt that this was not something that republicans would be involved in, particularly when the victim was a Catholic priest. The local IRA unit also stated that it had nothing to do with the attack.[11]

There were also attacks on farm animals by so-called republicans. One such attack took place in Kinturla, Kinvara, where a cow was savagely attacked with a razor or some sharp instrument and had its teats cut off. A bullock had its leg broken on the same farm.

Other incidents were less clear cut and may well have been the actions of republicans. In April, at Cloondarone near

Tuam, a girl was taken from her home by armed and masked men while her father and the rest of the family were held at gunpoint. They took her to backyard of the house where they cut her hair with shears. The terrified girl collapsed, but was shown no mercy. In fact, she was told that her ears would be cut off too. Her crime was allowing a young soldier to pay for a hobby horse ride for her niece while travelling amusements had been in Tuam earlier that day. The men did not question the girl as to how she knew the soldier – had they done so, she would have informed them that she had known him in Dublin and he had only lately been transferred to Tuam. She was surprised to see him and just spoke to him for a few minutes while the child took the ride on the hobby horse.[12]

These attacks reflected what was happening across the country at the time. Much of this brutality was caused by jealousy, greed and land grabbing and had absolutely nothing to do with the fight for freedom and the republic.[13] Such incidents are just a small example of what occurred during this violent period. All wars produce malicious and spiteful people who will stop at nothing to gain their own objectives, and Ireland was certainly no different.

The republican movement was well aware of the situation. By July 1920 several villages throughout Ireland had fallen under its control. The IRA rigorously enforced the rule of law in these places. They sought out men who had entered houses or businesses demanding money in the name of the Irish Republic and these men were severely dealt with in the republican courts.[14]

5

The Arrival of the
Black and Tans

The violence in 1919 convinced the British government that additional troops would have to be sent to Ireland to bring the country back under control. They would need to be ruthless in their attempts to defeat the IRA and subdue the Irish people. The first of a new group of English recruits began arriving in Ireland early in 1920, recruited by the British government, and were paid ten shillings per day – a princely sum at that time – to make Ireland a 'hell for the rebels'. There were not enough official police uniforms available for these new recruits, so they were dressed in a mixture of khaki and dark green. Some wore a khaki tunic and dark green trousers while others were dressed totally in khaki. Some had civilian hats, but most wore green caps, and the makeshift uniform was completed with a black leather belt. It was when they made their appearance in Limerick that they were immediately nicknamed the Black and Tans, after a once-famous pack of hunting hounds.

It has been claimed that the men were partly recruited

from prisons in Britain, although the British authorities stated that they were unemployed former soldiers, sent to Ireland to restore peace. However, the Black and Tans certainly never behaved like law enforcement officers – most were mere thugs and some were killers. Their actions managed to unite the Irish population like never before in defiance of British rule.[1] Although in Ireland for only a relatively short time, the Black and Tans managed to leave behind a deep legacy of hatred, equalled only by the Cromwellian wars of the seventeenth century. They were supported by an additional force called the Auxiliaries, made up for the most part of ex-British Army officers who had served in the First World War. The British government encouraged them to serve in Ireland by paying the Auxiliaries £1 per day, plus allowances. They were heavily armed and, granted free rein, many made the most of opportunities to loot and steal during raids.[2] The renowned IRA leader Tom Barry once said of them, 'of all the ruthless forces that occupied Ireland through the centuries, these Auxiliaries were surely the worst'.[3]

The arrival of the notorious Black and Tans in Galway was as disturbing for local people as it was for the Irish people countrywide. While the first of these new recruits were re-ported as arriving in Galway on 24 February 1920,[4] the of-ficial date was 24 March.[5] Those who arrived in Galway were noted leaving the station with all their equipment, including haversacks. They also had a prisoner with them – a young man named Michael Boyle, who had been arrested on firearms charges.[6] They took over the Railway Hotel for a short period, and a short time later took up residence in the police barracks in Eglinton Street, where they remained until the signing of the Anglo-Irish Treaty.[7]

Prior to the Black and Tans' arrival, Fr Dalton of St Mary's church in Carrick-on-Shannon had made an appeal to the IRA to cease the raids and attacks on the police as they were of no benefit. While he said that he would fully support such attacks if he felt it would help the Irish cause, he added, 'If the police were cast aside, the scum of the English towns would be brought over to take their place.'[8] It seems that he may have been aware of British government intentions.

The Tans continued to arrive in Ireland and by early October 1920 there were some 2,000 of them supporting an 8,000-strong RIC countrywide force.[9] Over 8,000 were eventually deployed to Ireland, and although the majority were British, some of them were Irishmen.[10] The new force was at an immediate disadvantage as its members were not familiar with their areas of occupation and depended on the RIC, informers and, of course, any available records pertaining to their district.

In Galway, while the RIC barracks held records on various republicans, the Customs House was also being used by police for storing information, which the authorities were now planning to hand over to the Tans. The building also held many other civil records that were important to the government. It was imperative that these records be removed. Galway IRA OC Seán Broderick took charge of this operation. Secrecy and speed were of the utmost importance and Broderick sent

Captain Seán Turke to check out the people living in the area and ensure that the military or police would not be informed of what was happening. A truck was secured to remove the boxes and files of records. A key was procured for the main entrance; a carpenter with a bit and brace looked after the remaining locks. During the operation, while the men were in the process of securing the records, a problem occurred outside. It is believed that the truck was spotted by the Tans and had to move off to avoid suspicion. Broderick and his men were left inside the building undetected, but when the danger had passed they were left with little choice but to destroy the records on the premises.[11]

The deployment of the Black and Tans in Ireland failed to have the desired effect. It was hoped that the IRA would be frightened into submission, but in fact they became more determined and attacks against British forces and other targets became more bitter, unpredictable and volatile.

The homes of the landed gentry had already been targeted for arms, but the earlier arms raids now escalated to violent attacks. On 3 March 1920, Frank Shawe-Taylor was shot dead at Coshla, a short distance from his home at Moorpark near Athenry. Shawe-Taylor was a large stock owner and was a regular visitor at the various fairs around Galway. He had left his home early that morning and although he employed a chauffeur, James Barrett, he sometimes drove the car himself. On this fateful morning, Barrett was sitting in the passenger seat. It was just after 6 a.m. and the morning was misty and cold. As the two men drove past Egan's pub in Coshla they noticed a cart broken down on the road some forty yards beyond the pub. When they reached the obstruction, Shawe-Taylor stopped the car and asked Barrett to move the cart off the road. While Barrett was moving the cart, a volley of shots rang out, and when Barrett turned he saw Shawe-Taylor slumped over in the car. The shots had come from behind a stone wall on the left side of the road. Barrett ran back to the car in an attempt to help Shawe-Taylor, who then uttered his last words and died of his wounds. Another shot rang out, hitting Barrett with shotgun pellets in the jaw as he dived behind the car for cover. Minutes later he heard the sound of footsteps as the assailants ran from the scene.

Barrett was terrified and remained lying on the ground for about ten minutes. He then heard movement from behind and someone helped him to his feet, at the same time warning him not to turn around. The man asked if he was badly injured and if he could walk. Barrett answered in the affirmative and was told to walk away and not look back. He reached the home of a family named Broderick who lived in the area and asked for help. A message was sent to Moorpark to inform Shawe-Taylor's wife of his death. She immediately set off to the scene of the ambush on a pony and trap, where she found her husband's lifeless body. The place was quiet and there was no one in sight. Barrett joined her a few minutes later and moved the body so he could drive the car. There was silence as the makeshift hearse travelled back to Moorpark. Apparently, about eight men took part in the ambush and it seems that Shawe-Taylor was shot at almost point-blank range as there were powder burns on the side of his face.

Frank Shawe-Taylor was a member of the Taylor family of Castletaylor near Ardrahan. A veteran of the Boer War and the Great War, he was described as a pleasant but somewhat condescending man. When it came to the distribution of land, he was unyielding and made it clear that he would never give up what he considered his land. He once said that if he was ever forced to hand over even part of his estate, he would only give it to ex-soldiers. He had received threats through the post regarding the allocation of land, but had ignored them. He also carried a loaded revolver: unluckily for him, he did not have it with him on the morning of the attack. An attempt had been made on his life a few years earlier, but he had escaped unharmed on that occasion. His funeral in Athenry was well attended by all sides of the community, but questions were left regarding his killing. Clearly it had been a deliberate assassination, but was it political or over the issue of land?[12]

Two months later a woman was shot during a raid for arms on Clydagh House, the home of the Lynch Staunton family near Headford. She was Harriet Murtagh, the housekeeper. Six men broke into the house and demanded that any guns be handed over. The housekeeper told them that there were no guns in the house, that they had been removed earlier, and she asked them to leave. One of the men pointed a shotgun at her, lowered it towards her legs and fired. She fell to the ground and was hit with 150 pellets at almost point-blank range. One of the shooter's companions challenged him and as he did so the owner of the house arrived on the scene from an adjacent room. He was armed and fired on the raiders. They returned fire, wounding Lynch Staunton, as they ran from the house. A short time later neighbours arrived and summoned the local doctor. This had been a ruthless attack on an unarmed woman and was condemned by all sections of the community.[13]

In June a party of four policemen, who were providing an escort for Mr G. Hutcheson and his two daughters, was attacked near Monivea. Hutcheson was a wealthy landowner with property in Ballybane and Monivea. At the time, the policemen were escorting Hutcheson and the girls to a religious service in Monivea. One of the daughters was driving the pony and trap, and two policemen cycled in front and two at the rear. Suddenly the peace of the morning was shattered as gunshots rang out. One of the policemen was wounded, but neither Hutcheson nor his daughters were hit during the incident.

The police and Hutcheson believed that the attack had nothing to do with politics but simply greed over land. Some months earlier a group of young men had approached Hutcheson's father and requested that sixty acres of his land be handed over to them. He had refused, and both he and his family had been placed under police protection.[14]

In July 1920 Sergeant Elliott from Ardrahan received a message that his wife was ill. The couple was living at the steward's lodge in Castletaylor at the time after receiving threats, and there was security in the grounds of the estate. Elliott went immediately to Castletaylor, taking a shortcut through some fields, and then headed towards the wooded area of the estate. In his haste to get to his wife, he had forgotten to take his gun. As he climbed over a stile close to the woods he was approached by two armed and masked men. One of them fired at him, but missed. However, the second man fired a shotgun, hitting Elliott in the arm, back and chest. The assailants then disappeared into the woods. Elliott managed to struggle on until he found help. He was taken to St Brides Home (a private hospital) in Galway, where he later recovered.[15]

That same month, two constables, Patrick Donnelly and Daniel Howley, were ambushed in Caltra near Ballinasloe.[16] Although they were seriously wounded, both men survived. There were a number of men arrested following the attack: Thomas Kilroy, Joseph Flynn, Patrick Kilcommins, Patrick Ruane, John Crosby and John Ryan. They were later taken to Renmore Barracks where they were court-martialled and sentenced to prison terms.[17]

***

During the initial stages of the war, the Tans and Auxiliaries believed that if they frightened and intimidated people enough, they would gather more information. However, this approach proved ineffective. They were more likely to come across information during raids by confiscating documents or by stopping suspects at random. One such incident occurred on the afternoon of Monday 22 March 1920, when Patrick

Fahy, an Irish teacher from Peterswell, was arrested while cycling through the village of Kilcolgan. It was believed that he had important republican papers with him and he was taken to the police barracks in Gort for questioning. On this same night the IRA attacked Castlegrove Barracks, but while there had been a mention of this barracks in the captured papers, it was too late to prevent the attack.[18]

Intimidation of the local population took many forms. The Tans and Auxiliaries were sometimes in the habit of swerving their vehicles towards pedestrians and cyclists to frighten them. In one incident near Oranmore, a woman and child had a narrow escape when a military lorry swerved towards them. It then skidded off the road and tumbled down a small embankment, injuring several of the soldiers, one of them seriously. One of the soldiers who escaped injury made his way to a nearby house and asked for a drink of water. After being looked after, he kicked the cup through the doorway.[19]

Throughout this time the Tans and Auxiliaries made their presence felt in many areas, raiding houses and businesses in the county as well as in the towns. On the night of 28 June, they raided suspected republican houses in Spiddal and arrested James and Joseph Thornton on firearm charges. Ammunition and a tricolour flag were confiscated. The flag was dragged at the back of the lorry while the prisoners were being taken to Galway Jail. John O'Rourke was arrested that same night after houses in the Oranmore and Maree area were raided. He was found in possession of two revolvers and ammunition and was also taken to prison.[20]

Once the authorities in Galway received information about republican safe houses or sympathisers, a raid would be planned. The strike was invariably at the most vulnerable time, mainly at night, taking advantage of the element of surprise. While the authorities mainly used their own vehicles during raids and other duties, they sometimes used public transport, depending on the distance. However, in June 1920 the railwaymen began to show their support for the republican cause by refusing to carry groups of armed police or military on the trains. The only train that was not affected by the refusal to carry armed police was the Galway to Clifden line, which would later prove fatal for Clifden (see Chapter 21).[21]

By July this situation had escalated and was affecting much of the public transport system around the country. The National Union of Railwaymen was called in to try to resolve the problem. After some meetings, the spokesman announced that the union had no objection to carrying unarmed police. Some train drivers began their own form of protest against the police and military by refusing to drive the train if any were on board, armed or unarmed. One such incident occurred after the police who were forced to vacate the barracks in Loughgeorge and Killeen made their way to Galway. From there they travelled to Athenry, where they were to change trains to complete their journey to Limerick. The train arrived on time but the driver refused to continue the journey if the police boarded. The situation became one of deadlock, and resulted in the passengers having to make their own way home.[22]

6

Galway Hunger Strike

Many of the men arrested during raids throughout the county ended up in Galway Jail. By April 1920 suspected republicans were being arrested and imprisoned without trial, and in response there was a series of hunger strikes. On Monday 12 April 1920, five IRA prisoners in Galway Jail began a strike. Two of the men were from Galway – Thomas Redington from the city and Thomas Duggan from Oranmore. The timing was significant and the men's actions attracted extensive publicity, as an eleven-day hunger strike by sixty-eight prisoners in Mountjoy Jail in Dublin had just ended with the prisoners, most of whom had also been interned without trial, being released. Their freedom had been gained with the support of a national strike of Irish workers across the country. To avoid a similar situation developing in Galway, political status was offered to the prisoners, which they refused, as their demand was to be released also.

When news of the Galway hunger strike reached the streets, a meeting was held by the labour movement and a general strike was planned for Galway on the following day. That night the town was plunged into darkness when the electricity workers shut down the supply. The Gashouse followed suit, causing panic among the people. The following morning pickets were placed on all shops and work establishments that attempted to open their premises. There were also rumours that the hunger strikers in Dublin had not been released and that some of them were in fact dead. The Dublin trains were not running, which caused alarm throughout the town. Sinn Féin held a public meeting in the Town Hall to inform people of the situation and to restore calm, and a temporary action committee was set up to disseminate information.

On Wednesday morning the streets of Galway were deserted – one reporter described it as looking like 'a city of the dead'. However, as the morning progressed, the streets became thronged with people looking for news. The town was virtually cut off from the outside world except for telegraph communication in the post office. Every house and business was closed and shutters were down everywhere: people were bracing themselves for what might happen if the prisoners were dead. Later that day another meeting was held in the Town Hall and it was announced that the rumours about the prisoners being dead were untrue, but they were still on hunger strike. Thus support for the prisoners continued. However, as people were running low on supplies in the town, it was decided by the temporary action committee that the flourmills, bakeries and butchers could resume work immediately. Once the shops received supplies, people purchased them, but they were only allowed immediate requirements – there was to be no hoarding of foodstuffs. Bars and hardware, fruit and vegetable shops had to remain closed.

An armoured car and army lorry arrived at Sullivan's butcher shop in William Street almost as soon as it opened and commandeered all of the meat for the army. The occupants then went to the grocery shop of J. J. O'Flynn in Woodquay and did the same, which inflamed the situation, as people were already enraged by the actions of the military. Later that day another armoured car travelled through the streets of the town with a soldier on observation duty mounted on top. The streets were busy with people, and as the soldier turned to look in one direction, he was hit on the head by a stone and knocked senseless, blood pouring from the wound. The culprit ran down Buttermilk Lane and escaped. The soldiers jumped from the armoured vehicle and ran through the crowded streets with fixed bayonets, causing more alarm. It was pointless giving chase, however, as there were huge crowds, and no one was going to reveal the identity of the man who had thrown the stone. Most of the witnesses were delighted by the assault and the soldiers knew this. They called off their search, having insulted and threatened some of the shoppers.

As the days passed, the situation strengthened the resolve of the Galway prisoners, who were aware of the support to be found outside the prison walls. The hunger strike continued for ten days and ended with the prisoners being released and taken to hospital until they were strong enough to go home. The first sign of the strike's end for the public was when the electricity was switched back on, amid great cheering. Victory for the prisoners was announced at the final public meeting, much to the delight of everyone present; the crowd almost immediately broke into patriotic songs. Labour leaders declared that the strike in Galway was the best conducted in Ireland and the town had never witnessed anything like this before. The solidarity and unity of the people was amazing; everything that needed 'to be at a standstill was exactly as it should be'.[1]

Another hunger strike began a few days later when John Furey and Michael Joyce, both from Oranmore, refused food while incarcerated in Galway Jail. They had been found guilty of having illegal arms in their possession and sentenced to one year's hard labour. They did not ask to be released, as they had been tried before a court, but they demanded to be treated as political prisoners. A week later a huge crowd gathered outside the jail in support of the prisoners' demands and Fr Michael Griffin, curate from Rahoon, led the people in reciting the rosary. Local Sinn Féin president L. E. O'Dea spoke out against the British government and warned them that the prisoners would prevail regardless. He said that 'John Bull' was discredited in every country in the world and would not be recognised again until 'he took his greedy claws off Ireland'. Speaking about the mothers of the hunger strikers, he said that in Oranmore there were staunch Irish women who said to their sons, 'Do not surrender; hold out to the end.' The republican solicitor George Nicholls also spoke at the gathering and warned the authorities that if Furey and Joyce died, then the people of Galway city and county would cry out for vengeance. Upon hearing this statement, the crowd erupted into loud cheering and applause. This hunger strike ended after seven days with the prisoners gaining political status.[2]

Among the other republicans who went on hunger strike was Michael Lynch. He was also given political status, but was held in prison. Originally from Connemara, he was a fluent Irish speaker and began teaching the language to other prisoners. Joyce was engaged to Tessie Traynor from St Bridget's Terrace in the city, whose brother James was also a member of the IRA. Tessie was a member of Cumann na mBan and during her fiancé's time in prison she often smuggled food and other commodities in to him. She was a girl of tremendous courage and many years later recalled the hunger strikes and the curfew imposed by the authorities. At night her home was plunged into darkness but, like other homes around the city, she blocked up the windows with turf and other objects so that she could keep a light on without attracting attention, which would bring the very real danger of shots being fired through the glass. Tessie and Michael Lynch eventually married and lived in St John's Terrace, Galway.[3]

While most would not readily admit it, there were some police officers who were prepared to let hunger strikers die. Lieutenant Colonel Gerald Bryce Ferguson Smyth, a divisional commander of the RIC in Munster, famously gave a statement openly acknowledging his stance in June 1920 in Listowel police barracks. The following extract from his declaration clearly shows his contempt for the republican movement, in particular hunger strikers:

If a police barracks is burned or if the barracks already occupied is not suitable, then the best house in the locality is to be commandeered, the occupants thrown into the gutter. Let them lie there, the more the merrier. Police and military will patrol the country at least five times a week. They are not to confine themselves to the main roads, but make across the country, lie in ambush and when civilians are seen approaching shout 'Up Hands'. Should the order not be obeyed at once shoot and shoot to kill. If the persons approaching carry their hands in their pockets, or are in any way suspicious-looking, shoot them down. You may make mistakes occasionally and innocent persons may be shot, but that cannot be helped, and you are bound to get the right person sometime.

The more you shoot, the better I will like you and I assure you no policeman will get into trouble for shooting a man.

Hunger-strikers will be allowed to die in gaol – the more the better. Some of them have already died and a damn bad job they were not all allowed to die. As a matter of fact some of them have already been dealt with in a manner their friends will never know about.

An emigrant ship left an Irish port for a foreign one lately with lots of Sinn Feiners on board; I assure you men it will never reach port.

Smyth was a Great War veteran and a native of Banbridge, County Down. Just one month after he made this statement he was in the County Club in Cork when a young IRA Volunteer walked up to him and said, 'Your orders were to shoot on sight. You are in sight now. So make ready.' Smyth was shot dead while trying to escape.[4]

7

Reprisals against Tuam

Statements such as Smyth's caused deep resentment and it was inevitable that hostility towards the police would increase throughout the country, particularly in the larger towns. Tuam and the surrounding areas had already experienced some violence, with attacks on police.

In July 1920 a daring attack took place in Bishop Street in Tuam when a number of police, accompanied by a military patrol, were shot at. Fire was returned, but no one was injured.[1] On 19 July a police patrol on its way from Galway to Dunmore was ambushed at Gallagh, some three miles beyond Tuam. Two of the constables, Carey and Burke, were shot dead while trying to take cover, having left the police van. The other two policemen returned fire, but were hopelessly outnumbered and forced to surrender after a fifteen-minute gunfight. Their weapons and ammunition were taken from them. The van was set alight after other weapons were removed from the vehicle. The two constables were then blindfolded and told to walk back towards Tuam.[2] The attack was carried out by some twenty men of the Barnaderg and Cortoon Companies, who were under the command of the Tuam Brigade OC Con Fogerty and his First Battalion commander Michael Moran.[3] It was later reported that over fifty men had taken part in the attack. After the alarm was raised, the Dragoon Guards from Claremorris and three lorry loads of police from Galway rushed to the scene of the ambush, but the attackers had already disappeared through the fields. The bodies of the dead policemen were taken to Vicar Street RIC Barracks in Tuam to await removal to their respective homes. At the time the barracks was occupied by about fifty policemen; these were now reinforced by the police from Galway.

A search of the attack area was ordered and took place throughout the evening and night for the ambushers, but no trace of them could be found. The night remained quiet until about 5 a.m., when the policemen arrived back from the search. The inhabitants of the town were suddenly awakened by the sound of gunfire. Tensions and tempers were high, and after viewing the bodies of their dead comrades the policemen had gone on a rampage through the town. What followed was described by a witness as follows: 'The Cathedral Town of Tuam with its peaceable population of under four thousand went through a perfect hell.' As the firing became more intense, it was accompanied by explosions. Screaming women and children ran to the rear of their premises and homes in terror, hoping to find safety there. At first, many people believed that the police barracks was under attack, but it soon became clear that the police were controlling the streets.

The Canney Brothers Drapery premises, located on the

corner of Vicar Street and the Dublin Road, was set alight while the family was upstairs. Luckily, the gunfire had woken them, so they were aware of the fire and able to react. Canney ushered his terrified wife and children down the stairs through the smoke. The hallway was already alight, but the family managed to reach the front door only to find the way out blocked by loaded rifles. In terror, they dashed back up the stairs, which were just beginning to burn, clambered out onto the back roof and made their escape. A short time later their home and business was gutted, and the Canneys lost all their belongings.

The Town Hall suffered a similar fate, and the sound of policemen cheering was heard as the building burned. The police also threw incendiary bombs into the grocery and provisions stores of John Burke and J. Nohilly further up the Dublin Road. Practically all business premises in Shop Street were damaged as police marched through the streets, smashing windows and doors with rifle butts. Other buildings were also set alight, causing much damage, and shots were fired through the upper windows of houses, where many people were hiding. According to one witness, it was a 'miracle' that no one was killed.

The police were aware of the location of at least one Sinn Féin member, John Neville, who was staying with a local woman in the town. A number of them, led by Constable Colleran, who had been in Tuam for a number of years, went directly to the house and demanded entry. Having gained access without having to force open the door, the policemen went upstairs and ordered Neville to come with them, saying, 'We are going to give you more mercy than you or your chums gave to my comrades.' Upon leaving the house, some of the other policemen wanted to shoot Neville and pointed their weapons at him, but Colleran persuaded them not to fire. Neville was held in custody for a number of hours and then released. He later remembered that during his ordeal he saw policemen carrying cans of petrol, which he believed were used to burn buildings in Tuam.

Another Sinn Féin member, Éamonn Casey, was also arrested that night. Policemen burst through the door and called him out, saying that they had orders to shoot. His wife, who was standing in the hall, implored them not to kill her husband. One of the policemen raised his rifle to hit her; he stopped when Casey asked them not to kill him in front of her. The head constable then intervened and ordered his men out of the house. Before releasing Casey, the policeman warned him that they would 'get' him within three weeks.

At this point the Dragoon Guards stationed in the town appeared on the streets, but when the officer saw what was happening he withdrew his men, saying that this was police business. The mayhem went on for well over an hour.

Once the gunfire and explosions stopped, people began leaving their homes to view the damage. They gathered together and organised themselves in a bid to combat the fires and save what little they could from the damaged buildings. Few houses escaped – windows were shattered and most buildings had between ten and thirty bullet holes in doors and ceilings. No place was safe that morning. Shots had been fired at the Convent of Mercy and other buildings outside Tuam had been attacked, including the Addergoole Sinn Féin hall, which was burned down. The RIC's behaviour was condemned by all sections of the community and in a sense overshadowed the killing of the two constables. The police claimed that they had been shot at first, and said that it had been while they were defending themselves that the mayhem had broken out.[4]

The Archbishop of Tuam, Dr Gilmartin, protested strongly to the authorities about the destruction of the town. While he condemned the killing of the policemen, he added that the town had been vengefully and ruthlessly sacked by the official guardians of the peace. This was not how the authorities should have handled the situation and he pointed out that such actions would only turn the vast majority of the population against the rule of law.[5] The police force admitted that some of their men had 'got out of hand', but asserted that they had been angered by the attack on their comrades and frustrated at the thought of justice not being served.

Over the following days a number of policemen said that they did not agree with the action taken by their colleagues. One of them, Constable Hugh Roddy, who was living in Bishop Street, Tuam, with his wife and children, resigned.[6] Shortly after his resignation the military paid a visit to his house and ordered him out of bed, saying, 'You're the man that left the night your comrades were murdered.' As he was being taken away, his wife tried to follow, but was ordered at gunpoint to get back. Roddy was taken by lorry to the home of Tommy Owens, the head porter at the railway station, who was also dragged out of his house in front of his terrified wife and children. The men were taken to a sandpit at Cloonascragh outside the town, where Roddy was ordered to strip. He was then beaten with leather belts and buckles and was punched and kicked as he tried to protect himself. Owens was forced to watch, after which he was taken to a wooded area near Ballinderry where he received the same brutal treatment. The two men later made their way back to Tuam, where they were looked after by neighbours. Similar attacks were made on a number of men that week.[7]

It was rumoured after this incident that the home of the Tuam Battalion OC Michael Moran was going to be burned by the Tans, so the house was guarded by the IRA, under the command of Captain Thomas Dunleavy of the Barnaderg Company, for a week. A number of months later Moran was arrested, but released shortly afterwards. However, he was then rearrested and taken to Galway city, where he was murdered by the Tans. His remains were brought home to Tuam for the funeral. The Volunteers marched unarmed with the hearse while the military tried without success to force them to break ranks. The Archbishop of Tuam and the parish priest protested and tried to stop the interference, but their appeals fell on deaf ears.

Following the funeral of Michael Moran, his friend Thomas Dunleavy was appointed as Tuam Battalion OC. Dunleavy had two brothers, Timothy and Patrick, in the IRA. Patrick served with the South Mayo Brigade before being appointed

OC of the North Galway Brigade. Timothy replaced his brother Thomas as captain of the Barnaderg Company.[8]

***

In August 1920, Sir Hamar Greenwood, the British Chief Secretary for Ireland, gave assurances in the House of Commons that within a few weeks the British Army, the Black and Tans and Auxiliaries would 'wipe out' all resistance to British rule in Ireland, by using aggressive force to achieve a victory over the republican movement and to regain complete control of Ireland for the British.[9] However, by later in the month his attitude had changed somewhat, as is evident from the following statement, which Greenwood made while addressing a parade of the RIC and Black and Tans in the Phoenix Park: 'Reprisals will ruin the discipline of the Force and cannot be countenanced by those in authority. There are cases where justifiable action has taken place, and these cases are being carefully investigated.' During his speech, Greenwood also mentioned his concern over the high number of men resigning from the RIC.[10] Perhaps the fate of Smyth, the previously mentioned Black and Tan divisional commander, and the unfavourable reaction to his speech by many of the RIC, had influenced attitudes going forward.

8

The Merlin Park Ambush and Reprisal

In August 1920 representatives of the various Galway companies of the IRA met at Michael Newell's forge in Brierhill. Those present included Brian Molloy, Thomas 'Baby' Duggan, Maurice Mullins, Michael Flaherty, Sonny King, Paddy King, Tom and John Mulryan, Dan, Bernard and John Fallon, and Ned and Pat Broderick. An ambush of the police at Oranmore was planned. Newell, who had had the police under surveillance for some time, reported that a sergeant and five or six constables usually travelled in single file from Oranmore to Galway on Saturdays between 9.30 and 10 a.m.[1] It was decided to attack the patrol on 21 August.[2] Sixteen men were detailed to take part in the ambush under the command of Brian Molloy. They met at the rear of Merlin Park House at 8.45 a.m. that morning and, armed with rifles and revolvers, made their way to the Dublin to Galway road.

The attack was to take place along the stretch of road near Roscam, close to the railway bridge (known locally as the Red

Bridge). Once the police passed under the bridge they were faced with a slight hill, bounded next to the railway bridge by a field and then woods. The first man was placed at the lower section of the field and the others took positions along the rising ground near the woods overlooking the route. Baby Duggan and Maurice Mullins took up positions on top of the railway bridge to prevent the enemy escaping back towards Oranmore. The orders were not to fire until the leader of the patrol was almost at the top of the hill, which meant that the full patrol would be well inside the ambush area.[3]

It was just after midday when the patrol arrived. It included Sergeants Mulhearn and Healy, the latter in charge, and Constables Brown, Patrick Doherty and Martin Foley. Doherty and Foley were about thirty yards ahead of the other three policemen. As the first two policemen reached the middle of the hill, the others passed under the bridge. Contrary to orders, the IRA men on the bridge opened fire on the policemen at the rear. At first the police were confused, as they could not see where the shots had come from and thought that it might be someone shooting at birds. Doherty and Foley were going around a slight bend in the road when Doherty spotted about ten men ahead of them. These were the men who had taken position on the rising ground, but on hearing the unexpected shots had moved down to find out what was happening. Doherty immediately shouted at Foley to turn back. They jumped from their bicycles and ran towards a gap in a stone wall leading to the woods. Shots rang out as they ran; seconds later a second volley was fired and Foley was hit. He fell to the ground and uttered his last words to his colleague: 'Paddy, I am done!' The other three policemen had also dismounted and had run for cover, but Constable Brown was shot and wounded. Despite this, they all managed to find cover behind the field boundary wall and returned fire.

Constable Doherty had escaped through the gap in the wall where his colleague lay dead and crawled through ferns and long grass, making his way through the woods to Renmore Barracks to raise the alarm. Sergeant Healy emptied his gun at the assailants as he moved along under the safety of the stone wall. He then ran to the railway line across the field as shots rang out after him, but he managed to reach the tracks and also headed towards Renmore Barracks. He reached the barracks a short time after Doherty. Meanwhile, back at Merlin Park, Sergeant Mulhearn made a dash for his bicycle and cycled towards Galway. As he did so, he received a gunshot wound to the back, but managed to keep going. He reached the town shocked and frightened, and received treatment for his wound.[4]

The gun battle at Merlin Park had gone on for about ten minutes when Brian Molloy ordered his men to call off the attack. It had not gone as planned – his men on the bridge had fired too soon. This had forced the main party to open fire before the policemen had actually reached the ambush location. After the attack the IRA collected the guns and bicycles left behind on the road by the police and reassembled in the wood. They felt sure that the Tans and Auxiliaries would search the area, and made their way back to Castlegar. It was a daring attack, considering Renmore Barracks was less than a mile away.[5]

When the alarm was raised, an armoured car and a lorry load of troops left Renmore Barracks, led by a Scottish Air Force officer on a motorcycle. By the time they got to the scene, the place was silent; Constable Foley was lying dead near the gap leading into the woods, his revolver and bicycle missing. Two very frightened girls, the daughters of John Leech, the assistant town clerk, who lived nearby, arrived. They told the officer commanding that another policeman had staggered into their avenue and collapsed, and that he was just lying in the avenue, bleeding. There was nothing they could do for him. The army motorcyclist left the area at full speed to summon an ambulance and a priest. The ambulance arrived a short time later and took Constable Brown away. The priest, Monsignor Considine, administered the last rites to Constable Foley. Police also arrived to secure the area.[6]

A young girl named Eileen Lyons passed the scene as she made her way to Galway, with a friend, on a pony and trap. A large group of soldiers, police and Tans, all armed, was on the scene. A pool of blood was clearly visible on the road. As they stabled the pony in Prospect Hill, the girls were warned not to spend too long in the town, as Oranmore, where they had come from, was to be 'sacked' by police that night. The girls took the advice and returned home as quickly as possible to warn their families. Some people were already aware that an attack was imminent and had left for safer locations in the countryside.[7] Fr Casey went to the police to try to reason with the constables, asking them to remain calm and saying that two wrongs would not make a right. Although the policemen were vengeful, they gave Fr Casey the impression that there would be no reprisals.[8]

Nevertheless, tensions were high as night fell. A young man named Higgins was attacked and beaten by police in Dominick Street in Galway city while making his way home to the Claddagh. He managed to escape by running down Nun's Island. There were a number of other men attacked in the Dominick Street area that night, but although several shots were fired, no one was hit.[9] Another man named Kavanagh was severely beaten about the head. At about 10 p.m. the police stopped a car on its way from Salthill and while they were questioning the driver a small crowd gathered. Two of the onlookers standing at the back of the crowd shouted, 'Up Roscam, up Oranmore!' The police turned and hushed the crowd, but were unable to catch the young men, who made good their escape, running down Raleigh Row.[10]

At about 11 p.m. a large number of police and Tans arrived in Oranmore, bent on revenge, and began a series of attacks on business premises and houses. They were supported by the Auxiliaries, who arrived from Galway in Crossley Tenders. Many of them were drunk.[11] The Tans surrounded Keane's public house and general store where Joe Howley lived and called on him to surrender. Howley had already gone on the run that evening, as he knew that he would be sought out: IRA meetings had been held in Keane's, so he was an obvious target. The police and Tans began shooting into the premises and Howley's mother and stepfather had to vacate the building,[12] which the Tans then set alight, reducing it to a burned-out shell in a short time.[13] A little later, they turned their attention to the buildings across the road from the pub, including the local Sinn Féin hall. A man named Brian Coen, his wife and three young children lived in an adjoining cottage. The shootings and explosions terrified the family, in particular the children, who could hear one of the policemen shouting, 'Fire again boys, give them plenty of it!' The hall was set alight and the fire spread to the Coens' cottage, but as the family tried to get out the front door they were confronted by armed men who forced them back into the burning house. Luckily, they were able to escape through the back door.

Other houses were attacked and windows and furniture smashed. As bombs were exploding there was wild cheering and one of the Tans shouted, 'This is only the beginning; Castlegar will get it next night!' Most people either remained huddled in the backs of their homes or sought refuge in the fields behind the village.[14] The house of Thomas Lee was also attacked and about twelve shots were fired through a window. Lee received a slight leg wound as he dashed up the stairs. Looking out of the bedroom window, he saw that a body of police had taken up positions in front of the house. He then made his way out through the backyard and ran through the fields, where he remained until morning.[15] Eileen Lyons and her mother took refuge in the Costello family home, next to the Band Hall, as they felt it would be safe there, but the hall was set alight and they were forced to flee. Eileen and her mother decided to return home, and the Costello family joined them in the dash for safety. As they ran in panic, Eileen became separated from the others. When she ran past the blazing building, the Tans ordered her to stop. Terrified, she ignored their orders, and they opened fire on her, but missed. She eventually found the others again and they took shelter in a vacant house next to their own.

Despite the danger around the village, some men, women and children formed a human chain, passing buckets of water in an effort to save some of the houses. Furniture that had been saved from the flames was stored on the roadside, but the Tans weren't finished – they riddled family possessions with bullets.[16]

Gunfire and bomb blasts continued into the early hours of the morning. The arrival of British officers and airmen who were stationed in nearby Oranmore aerodrome brought a degree of hope, as they tried to bring about order and quench the fires started by their comrades.[17]

Elsewhere around the country that night there were a number of attacks on police. Among the victims was Sergeant Thomas Craddock, a native of Ballinasloe, who was mortally wounded as he left the Great War Club in Athlone.[18] People in Castlegar were rightfully extremely worried about a reprisal the next night, but it did not happen.

The ambush at Merlin Park had not been authorised by Seamus Murphy, OC of the Galway Brigade of the IRA, and when he became aware of it he was furious and threatened to have the men responsible court-martialled. However, he took into consideration the records of the men involved and decided against this action. Shortly after the ambush, the Galway Brigade was divided into three sections to try to ensure greater control over the men. The First Battalion, with Brian Molloy as its OC, consisted of seven companies: Galway City, Castlegar, Cussaune, Monivea, Derrydonnell, Newcastle and Cregmore; the Second Battalion, Patrick Feeney OC, consisted of four companies: Claregalway, Annaghdown A, Annaghdown B and Kilcoona; the Third Battalion consisted of three companies: Clooneen, Claren and Caherlistrane.[19]

9

Lancers Targeted

In July 1920 *The Evening Standard* reported that 'mysterious airplanes' had been seen flying over the west of Ireland, manned by Sinn Féiners wearing British uniforms. The aeroplanes were believed to be surplus military machines from the Great War, which were being sold off. The British government then placed an embargo on the sales of such aircraft to Ireland.[1] It is difficult to believe that such reports were even entertained as possible by the government, let alone acted upon.

Nationalists had decided to create their own embargo the previous month, when a boycott of the police had been ordered by the republican movement:

> Notice is hereby given that intercourse of any kind whatsoever is strictly forbidden between citizens of the Irish Republic and that portion of the Army of Occupation known as the RIC; that a general boycott of the said force is ordered, and that you will cease as from June 29, 1920, to transact any business of any nature whatsoever with the said force. All persons infringing this order will be included in the said boycott. By order, Competent Military Authority, June 28, 1920, A.D.[2]

This led to many Galway business people not wishing to deal with the military, some out of fear, but most out of a sense of duty to their country.

In July 1920 the Galway Lawn Tennis Club was attacked and burned down by members of the IRA. All the tennis equipment was consumed in the fire and six tennis courts were dug up, as was the croquet ground. The fencing that surrounded the playing area was broken and the seating on either side of the courts was piled onto the blazing building. The club members were appalled at the arson attack and one member stated that he 'could not conceive that the burning had any political significance'. During a meeting of Galway Urban Council the following week, the chairman said:

> I have no sympathy with the class exclusion of the people who use that club, nor indeed with the company they keep, but at the same time I think the burning is simply an act of pure vandalism. Talking to the people of the town I find they generally condemn the act. I do not think it necessary for me to go into the matter very fully, but you remember that a month or fortnight ago we referred certain matters of thieving that was going on in Salthill to the Volunteers, and I understand that recently the perpetrators of these robberies have been brought to book and are punished.

The Urban Council referred the burning of the tennis club to the 'republican police' and while they acknowledged the letter and promised to investigate the matter, the identity of those responsible was never revealed.[3] Seán Broderick later stated the club was targeted because it was perceived to be a 'favourite meeting place of British military officers', among them officers of the Sixth Dragoon Guards (known as the Lancers in Galway). Also destroyed that night were various pieces of military equipment, barbed wire and feed for the Lancers' horses at Earls Island.[4]

At midnight on 13 August 1920, shots were fired in the vicinity of Earls Island, where the Lancers were stationed in a military camp situated close to University College Galway. It was believed that the shots came from the railway bridge spanning the River Corrib and were aimed at the barracks. Following the exchange, the Dragoons left their barracks in force. All were mounted on horseback and they began patrolling the streets of the town. The only people they came across during that night were members of the Flintoff–Moore Opera Company who were on their way to the railway station after giving a performance in the Town Hall. Despite the strong military presence in the streets that night, the authorities were annoyed and surprised to find a tricolour mounted over the Town Hall the following morning. It was secured to the mouth of the large stone lion which formed part of the royal coat of arms.[5] One reason for the attack on this barracks was that IRA prisoners were sometimes taken to the Earls Island camp for interrogation and could be held there for days without being handed over to the courts or the jail authorities.

The prisoners were kept in semi-circular huts at the Earls Island camp. Conditions were terrible during winter as there was no heating. One soldier was caught giving an inmate a blanket and was stopped by an officer, who said that he never heard of swine needing blankets. It was here that Michael Moran from Tuam was shot dead, just behind the old college handball alley. One witness later stated that she once saw a Crossley Tender full of prisoners arriving with the Tans, who were 'howling like devils'. The Tans had taken the prisoners from Barna and thrown them into the nearby river. When they crawled out, they were taken, dripping wet and cold, directly to be imprisoned in the 'doghouse' huts.[6]

Another man held prisoner and almost killed at the Earls Island camp was Tom Courtney from Newcastle. Courtney was born in a house on Newcastle Road in 1890, and became a prominent IRA man with the Galway Company, having initially taken an interest in Irish nationalist politics after hearing Arthur Griffith speak at Eyre Square. A number of people had gathered to listen to Griffith but were encouraged to move on by two RIC men, one of whom knew that Courtney worked for the post office and asked him if he should be at work. Courtney moved on, but he never forgot Griffith's speech. As a teenager he had begun working as a telegraph boy in the Galway post office and as such was in the ideal job to double as an intelligence officer in the republican movement – this work involved intercepting mail belonging to the military in Renmore Barracks and the RIC throughout Galway city and county. The department was code-named the 'steaming and opening department'. (For years, Courtney's son David believed that such a department actually existed!)

Courtney's IRA code name was Captain Puzzle. His duties also included delivering republican documents and letters to the various local commanders during his normal postal deliveries. However, while carrying out this duty in Castlegar, a hotbed of republican activity at the time, Courtney was stopped by the Black and Tans and searched. Upon discovering IRA documents, which Courtney denied any knowledge of, the Black and Tans arrested him and took him to the military barracks at Earls Island for questioning. During the interrogation, he was handcuffed and tied with a rope before being thrown into the river close by. He somehow managed to stay afloat until he was pulled out. They then threw Courtney into a hole dug close to the river bank and shovelled clay on top of him as if to bury him alive, but his nerve held and after a few minutes he was pulled from the hole and thrown into a cell, still wet and covered in mud. He knew that he faced certain death if he admitted his involvement with the IRA.

Messages were smuggled in to Courtney by an altar boy, who slipped him notes concealed under the paten during Holy Communion. When Courtney was eventually released from Earls Island, he was hesitant about leaving, fearing that he might be shot in the back on the pretext that he was trying to escape. This was known to have happened to some republicans. Nevertheless, he took his chances, left his confinement and then went on the run. During this time his wife, like those of other on the run republicans, was looked after financially by the IRA. Finance was also made available to support the families of such men. This was sometimes done through a sympathetic priest, who could pass on the money on the pretext of hearing confession.

Due to the absence of the men, during the regular raids carried out by the authorities, it was the women who bore the brunt of the abuse. Any incriminating equipment and documents had to be disposed of quickly. During one raid on the Courtney home in Newcastle, a large quantity of medical items and some incriminating material had to be hidden urgently. Tom's mother gathered up the items and brought them out the back of the house. As there was so little time before the authorities arrived, she disposed of them by throwing them over the next door neighbour's wall. This was the home of an RIC man whose family, luckily, was obviously sympathetic to the Irish cause. Following the raid, the man's wife returned the discarded items, saying, 'I think these belong to you.'[7]

Later in August, the Dragoons were forced to evacuate their quarters in Earls Island when Richard MacNevin, bailiff for Galway and armed with a writ, evicted them. The shocked commander and his troops had just finished breakfast when the order was served. The land was formally occupied by the Green Marble Company and the landlord was owed over £654. It was reported that this was the first time in the history of Ireland that any section of the 'Army of Occupation' had been evicted from a premises. The military obeyed the law and evacuated the buildings, and although they did regain control of the premises some time later, such treatment of the British was a sign of the changing times, and reflected changing policies and opinions in Ireland.[8]

10

Night of Terror

A British officer who was sympathetic to the nationalist cause had arrived in Galway a few days before the Merlin Park ambush in August 1920. Pat Margetts from Oxford was a Great War veteran who had served with a Scottish regiment and seen much action during the war, including at the Somme. He was therefore no stranger to trouble.

Before his arrival in Galway, Margetts had been stationed in Belfast, where he and his company had been given the task of protecting the Catholic church and convent of St Matthew in Ballymacarrett. In his own words, he witnessed 'all the terrible excesses of the Orange mob' during the fury of the anti-Catholic pogrom of July 1920. He was, therefore, not sorry to learn that he was to be transferred. The location of his next tour of duty was kept secret at first, before he was told that he and his company were being sent to a 'very pleasant', friendly place in the west of Ireland. The journey from Belfast to Galway was accomplished on foot in full marching order and gear. The men avoided the main roads as much as possible, marched south and experienced glorious sunshine throughout the journey. Upon hearing frightening stories at every police barracks they reached, they could not help but wonder where all these 'rebels' were – they had encountered nothing but kindness and hospitality on the journey to Renmore Barracks. Upon arrival, Margetts immediately made friends with some of the local people and took an instant liking to his new post. During the following days, known members of Sinn Féin were pointed out to him and his colleagues. Their initial uncertainty about reports of trouble and shooting in the south was about to be challenged.[1]

On the night of 8 September 1920, Seán Broderick was making his way to Galway Railway Station to meet Michael Thornton from Spiddal, who was to arrive on the late train from Dublin. As Broderick approached the station he heard shots and rushed towards the entrance. He arrived to find two men – Seán Mulvoy, a twenty-year-old member of the IRA, and Constable Edward Krumm, who some believed was a Black and Tan – lying mortally wounded. Krumm was not in uniform on the night he was killed, but it seems some time earlier he and a number of other Tans had been drinking in Baker's Hotel, Eyre Street.[2] One of the men he was with that night was Charles Yorke, a chauffeur from Dublin, who was staying at the hotel. The two men had been discussing horse racing, as the St Leger had been run that day. Krumm had had a bet on a horse named Spion Cop and wondered if it had won the race. Both men then made their way to the station to meet the midnight train and find out, as the morning newspapers were usually on this train.[3]

There was a crowd of people waiting, most for the arrival of the newspapers, but they were mostly interested in the story of Terence MacSwiney's hunger strike. The train pulled in as normal and after it came to a stop the porters opened the baggage car. There had not been enough newspapers to meet demand on the previous nights and as soon as unloading began the people surged forward. When Krumm saw the people rushing along the platform, he drew his gun and began intimidating them. He does not appear to have fired any shots in the station, but once outside he fired two or three shots into the air. There are various accounts of what happened next. Some say that he took deliberate aim at Seán Mulvoy and shot him through the head, after which the crowd rushed him and knocked him to the ground. As Krumm was trying to aim his gun at his assailants, someone stepped forward and shot him. It was also said that Mulvoy attempted to disarm Krumm by jumping on his back, but Krumm managed to point the gun over his shoulder and fire, mortally wounding his attacker.[4]

According to most sources the other IRA men at the scene that night were Seán Turke and Frank O'Dowd. Both were also involved in the fracas that resulted in the shooting of Krumm.[5] It was rumoured afterwards that it was a bullet from O'Dowd's revolver that killed Mulvoy, but this was denied by all the witnesses.[6]

There are other versions of the story, one of which states that the man who killed Krumm was Thomas Mahony from Killeenadeema. According to this story, Mahony shot Krumm in the chest, and, as he fell to the ground, Krumm managed to fire off one shot, hitting the IRA man in the leg, a few inches above the knee. Mahony was immediately taken by his colleagues to a safe house where his wound was quickly dressed. The owner of the house was an old lady, a republican sympathiser. They prepared a horse and cart and, dressed as the old lady, Mahony was taken to a private hospital in Salthill. The following day he was warned that the Tans were searching hospitals for him. He asked a nurse to get word to the IRA that he was in danger. A short time later, Mahony was taken by boat to Maree, where he was met by other republicans and taken across the countryside, avoiding the roads, to Killeenadeema, where he was hidden and looked after by relatives until he recovered.[7]

Another variation records that Krumm had spent the evening drinking and arrived at the station drunk. That same night the Volunteers were also meeting the train to collect weapons. They stopped the train outside the station and removed the guns. The train was then driven into the station and as passengers began to disembark and leave the platform Krumm drew his gun and aimed it at the crowd. It was then that Seán Turke jumped onto his back in an attempt to overpower him. Seán Mulvoy went to help Turke, but Krumm managed to fire his weapon a number of times, killing Mulvoy and wounding another man. Another Volunteer arrived on the scene and shot Krumm. According to this version, Mulvoy was taken to his lodgings, where he died on arrival, but this is contradicted by a report from the County Infirmary.[8] Krumm's companion Charles Yorke later stated that after they had got the newspapers, he had left the station ahead of Krumm. Suddenly, he heard a shot being fired and before he could do anything an armed man was standing in front of him, pointing his gun and telling Yorke to put his hands up. Yorke attested that another man came from behind and searched him. As he was standing there, he heard a man calling for help, and then heard Krumm say, 'If you do not let me go, I will fire.' The man who was searching him then left, after which Yorke heard a number of shots. When he turned, there were two men lying on the ground bleeding: Krumm and Mulvoy.[9]

These differing versions of how the shooting began and the events that followed prove how difficult it is to get accurate information, even from eyewitnesses. The only certain fact is that both Mulvoy and Krumm were killed that night. Both were taken to the County Infirmary in Prospect Hill, where Krumm died almost immediately and Mulvoy lived for almost two hours. Seán Mulvoy had been living in Bohermore at the time and worked as a shop assistant in Corbett's Hardware Store in Williamsgate Street.

The Black and Tans stationed in Eglinton Street and the Auxiliaries from Lenaboy reacted immediately and set out for revenge. They fired volleys of shots at houses and businesses throughout the town – shop windows and doors were prime targets. The City of the Tribes resounded with rifle fire and exploding grenades as the Tans went on the warpath. Many houses were raided and the occupants were roughly forced out onto the streets in nightclothes, while Tans sprinkled petrol, attempting to burn properties.[10]

At about 2.30 a.m. the Tans made their way past Eyre Square to the home of Seán Broderick in Prospect Hill.[11] He had returned home shortly after leaving the station and was asleep in bed when the Tans arrived. He awoke to hear his father shouting from downstairs. Seán's room was at the top of the house, so he had no means of escape. His mother and sister, Peg, were also in the house that night. The Tans pushed his father aside and ran up the stairs, grabbing Seán, who had dressed in a shirt and trousers. They pulled him down the stairs, not allowing him time to put on his shoes, and dragged him out onto the street, setting the house alight and shouting abuse at Broderick, who was then marched towards the railway station. The Tans were hitting him with their rifles. Broderick called to a British officer that as an officer of the Irish Republican Army he was entitled to and demanded a fair trial. The officer replied, 'You bloody Bastards didn't give much of a trial to the policeman last night.'

Broderick was taken to the far end of the station and pushed up against a large wooden door. The Tans stood back and took up positions as a firing party. Moments later, the officer commanding gave orders to fire. The only words that Broderick heard as he closed his eyes, expecting to die, were, 'Present … Fire!' He later stated that he uttered a prayer to the Blessed Virgin, which he believed saved his life. He felt a sharp sensation on the top of his head and fell to the ground, blood splattering from the wound. Although he immediately realised that he wasn't seriously injured, he began to moan and kick for a moment, and then suddenly went silent. He lay perfectly still and, believing that he was dead, the Tans left the area without any further shots being fired. Broderick lay for a while until he felt that it was safe to move, then got to his feet and staggered to a safe house. While he never knew how many shots were fired, he was only hit by one bullet, which skimmed across the top of his head, cutting the skin to the bone, but failing to penetrate his skull. An attempt to burn his house had also failed, as neighbours helped quench the flames after the Tans had left. Broderick returned home the following morning to collect some belongings and then went on the run to south Mayo, where he served with a number of companies under Commandant Tom Maguire.[12]

It was to prove a long and dangerous night in Galway. At about 3 a.m. the Tans and Auxiliaries burst through the door of Madden's lodging house in St Brendan's Terrace, Woodquay. Armed police surrounded the premises, making sure that no one could escape. Four armed men ran upstairs to the bedroom where Thomas Fahy and Joe Cummins were sleeping. Both young men worked in Brennan's Drapery in the town. They were quickly roused out of their sleep, and as Fahy dressed he was hit over the head and knocked against the bedroom wall. There was a shout from below stairs – 'Wait for orders!' – which it seems saved him. Cummins was dragged down the stairs, where the officer asked his men, 'How many have you got?'

'Two,' came the reply.

'One will do this time,' the officer said and Cummins was taken away. Two of the Tans re-entered the bedroom and told

Fahy that he would be spared until another night. Cummins was also taken to the railway station, where he was also shoved up against the large doorway of the parcel office. The order 'Ready ...' was given. Cummins knew exactly what was coming, and just as the officer called out 'Fire!' he dived to the ground, with most of the volley passing over his head. Although he was hit by one bullet in the leg, he lay perfectly still. Moments later he heard one of the soldiers saying that they should fire another volley into him, but another replied, 'Leave the bastard there, he's finished.' Believing he was dead, the soldiers moved away towards the town. Cummins lay still for a time after they left. A short while later two soldiers from another regiment arrived on the scene. One of them shoved Cummins with his boot and asked the other if he was dead. In the hope of getting assistance, Cummins replied, 'No.' The soldier replied, 'You soon will be,' and they both walked away. Cummins crept away and, under the cover of darkness, made his escape. Like Broderick, he was extremely lucky – the following morning, station staff counted twelve bullet holes in the door.[13]

The military continued their hunt for IRA men that night. Seamus Quirke was a young jeweller who worked for Jeremiah O'Donovan in Williamsgate Street. He was a known member of the IRA and rented a room at the home of Charles Burbidge and his wife on the Dock Road. At about 4.30 a.m. armed and uniformed Tans and Auxiliaries called to the Burbidge home. The servant girl who slept downstairs went to the door and asked who was knocking. She was requested to open the door immediately. The girl asked for time to get dressed and call Mrs Burbidge, but again was told to open the door immediately. Before she could do anything, Mrs Burbidge, who was already awake, rushed down the stairs. Upon opening the door she was met by the barrels of rifles.

'We want Quirke,' one of the men called out. 'Where is he?'

Mrs Burbidge, hoping to delay them, asked if she could get a light.

'We want no light. Quirke is the man we want.'

They pushed past her while she was trying to light the lamp and ran upstairs, calling out for Quirke, who asked for time to get dressed. They gave him two minutes, but as he was pulling on his trousers, they started to push him out of the room, so he grabbed his rosary beads. Dressed only in a shirt and trousers, he was forced from the house in his bare feet and brought along the quay towards the old Gashouse. His rosary beads were pulled out of his hands and thrown into the water. About 300 yards from his lodgings, he was made to stand under a lamp post, where he was surrounded by ten of his captors. They opened fire, hitting Quirke nine times in the stomach and once in the back. They then walked away, leaving him for dead. However, he was still alive, and after they had gone made his way back towards the Burbidge home with the help of some Connemara fishermen. He asked for a priest and one was summoned immediately.

Once home, Quirke was placed on a makeshift stretcher in the parlour, and even through his intense pain apologised to Mrs Burbidge for causing such trouble at her home. 'I am dying now,' he said and asked her to pray for him. Quirke was gently carried upstairs and lifted onto a bed, crying out in pain and bleeding profusely. Mrs Burbidge asked him if she could do anything for him. He replied that she was too kind, but asked if she would let her little seven-year-old daughter, Lilian, pray with him. He had a great bond with the little girl, and as his life ebbed away she knelt and prayed beside his bed. Fr Griffin arrived just in time and administered the last rites.[14] Doctor William Sands was also summoned, but there was nothing he could do to keep Quirke alive. He died moments later.[15] According to one source, a man named Sergeant Fox was responsible for the murder of Seamus Quirke.[16]

The night of terror in Galway only ended because the British Army intervened. An urgent message had been sent to Renmore Barracks requesting immediate military assistance in the town. Troops were hastily dispatched under the command of Pat Margetts. It was reported that the police barracks in Eglinton Street was under siege. Margetts was shocked at the actions of the Tans and Auxiliaries and while he stopped the destruction of property, he was too late to prevent the shootings.[17]

11

Funerals and Inquests

The following afternoon, 9 September, at about 5 p.m., the offices of the *Galway Express* newspaper at Eyre Square were attacked by the Tans and Auxiliaries, who smashed all of the machinery and furniture, causing as much damage as possible.[1] The reason for the attack was possibly that the newspaper had published a leaflet that morning regarding the murders and mayhem of the previous night.[2] The premises of Thomas Walsh, a grocer and publican, were then set upon and doused with petrol, but before the buildings could be set on fire troops from Renmore Barracks arrived. Commanding officer Pat Margetts ordered the men to stop the destruction and return to their respective barracks.[3] One of the Auxiliaries refused to obey the orders and struck the match regardless. Margetts drew his revolver and pointed it at the Auxiliary officer's head, saying, 'If you drop the match, you won't live to see it light.' The soldier reluctantly but carefully quenched the match and ordered his men to return to barracks.[4]

It seems that the Tans and Auxiliaries were intent on burning all of the buildings around Eyre Square that evening.

Luckily, the intervention of the army seemed to calm the situation and, with the exception of a few shots fired later that night, the town was relatively quiet.[5] One reason for this was that a curfew had been imposed that day between the hours of 9 p.m. and 4 a.m. No one was allowed on the streets between these hours without a permit. Orders were issued to arrest anyone who disobeyed these regulations, and a shoot-to-kill policy was to be put into effect if anyone refused to halt or resisted arrest. People could not even have interior lights on during these hours. It was also announced that about 150 extra Black and Tans had been drafted into the town after the shootings.[6]

The funeral masses of Mulvoy and Quirke took place together in the pro-Cathedral at 10.45 a.m. on Friday 10 September 1920. All work was suspended in Galway that morning and people gathered in churches throughout the city and offered prayers and communion for the dead men. The pro-Cathedral was packed long before the mass began and places had to be set aside for the families of the deceased. These included Mulvoy's two sisters (his father and mother were dead) and Quirke's father, Christopher. Thousands failed to gain admittance and gathered in the streets outside. Some forty priests, including Fr Michael Griffin, attended, and the chief celebrant was the Bishop of Galway, Dr Thomas O'Dea. Both coffins were draped in tricolours and surrounded by lighted candles. The inscription on the breastplate of Seamus Quirke's coffin read: 'Seamus Quirke, Adjutant, A Coy., 1st Batt., 1st Galway Brigade, IRA, Aged twenty-three years.

Murdered by England's police spies. September 8, 1920 – RIP.' Seán Mulvoy's coffin carried a similar inscription. Men and women wept openly as the priests sang in unison, rising as if in a triumphal cry and lowering to almost a murmur.

When the service concluded, the highly polished oak coffins, still draped in tricolours, were carried from the church. Quirke's cap and Volunteer uniform were placed on top of his coffin. As the fife and drum band began playing the 'Dead March', the mournful procession moved off. The band was followed by the bishop and his assembly of priests. The hearse then followed, accompanied by members of the IRA. The women of Cumann an mBan took their place also and some 10,000 people followed the funeral as it made its way to St James' Cemetery in Mervue where Seán Mulvoy was to be buried. From there the remains of Seamus Quirke would be taken to his native Cork. The funeral cortège took a route through Middle Street, Cross Street, Mainguard Street, Shop Street, William Street around by Eyre Square and up through College Road. It then passed the small house where Mulvoy was born. Thousands lined the route and shutters and blinds were down in every business and home as a mark of respect. When the funeral procession reached the little cemetery in Mervue, the remains of Seamus Quirke were transferred to a waiting motor vehicle, which was guarded by members of the IRA while the burial of Seán Mulvoy took place. The IRA lined up two deep in the cemetery as relatives, clergy, friends and sympathisers crowded around the grave. The graveside service then took place, after which a volley was fired.[7] There was a military presence and photographs were taken of IRA members, which were later disposed of by Pat Margetts in case of more killings.[8] The second funeral then carried on south, accompanied by Quirke's father, Christopher, several friends and members of the IRA. Quirke's mother had been unable to make the trip to Galway as she was extremely ill and hospitalised at the time. In fact, Quirke should not have been in Galway on the night he was killed, as he had planned to go home to visit his mother, but then had postponed the journey for two days.

Seamus Quirke's burial took place in St Finbarr's Cemetery on Sunday 12 September 1920. As in Galway, thousands turned out to pay their respects to the young Volunteer. Various bands, organisations and members of the IRA from units throughout Cork took part in the solemn procession to the cemetery. The lord mayor of the city, Terence MacSwiney, who was himself dying on hunger strike, sent messages of condolence to the family. One of the priests, Fr Dominick, in a letter to Quirke's parents stated: 'I am glad your son's remains are laid to rest in the heroes' plot where he is the first battalion officer, and I fear more will soon be laid to rest.'[9]

On 11 September 1920, the remains of Edward Krumm were taken under police and military escort to Galway Railway Station for the first stage of a journey to London for burial.[10] There was little sympathy among the people of Galway for Krumm – they were more interested in knowing the facts about that night. A Public Commission of Inquiry was set up in the Town Hall a week after the shootings, to be chaired by Monsignor Considine. It comprised members of the legal profession and the chairman of Galway County Council. There were a number of witnesses and a large crowd was in attendance. As proceedings got under way, District Inspector Richard Cruise and Head Constable Daly walked into the room and approached Monsignor Considine. Cruise told him that the Commission of Inquiry was illegal and they would have to stop proceedings: this, he stressed, was a military order and there were troops outside ready to enforce these orders if necessary. There was a heated discussion, during which Monsignor Considine protested in the strongest possible terms, as did a number of others, but the police reiterated that they would use force, if necessary, to clear the hall. Monsignor Considine then reminded the others that the authorities would use violence if their orders were not obeyed. However, one of the legal team, L. O'Dea, dismissed Cruise and went to address that crowd, saying: 'Ladies and Gentlemen, we are about to hold an inquest into the terrible murders … We wanted a full frank inquiry and the police do not want that.' He was interrupted immediately by Cruise. Fearing that innocent people might be hurt, O'Dea stopped for a moment, then thanked the people for attending and asked them to disperse quietly. There was much anger in the streets over the commission being declared illegal.[11]

The military decided to hold its own inquiry with hand-picked witnesses. It opened in Renmore Barracks on 10 September 1920. Major Yeldham (Connaught Rangers) presided, and other members of the inquiry included Captain

J. V. Preston Whyte (Dragoon Guards), Captain E. Lynsday Young (Connaught Rangers) and Head Constable Daly. Daly described Krumm as a twenty-five-year-old unmarried native from London, of steady temperate habits, who appeared to be a respectable man.

Eileen Baker of Baker's Hotel was the first person called to give evidence. She said that she had known Edward Krumm for about a month, that he sometimes had his lunch in the hotel and that he liked to play billiards. On the night in question, Constable Krumm and Charles Yorke were in the hotel until about 11.45 p.m., when they left for the station together. Daly asked her about the condition of the men when they left her premises. She replied that both of them were perfectly sober and told the inquiry that Charles Yorke returned at about midnight in a panicked state. He said to her, 'He's gone, he's dead.'

'Who?' she asked.

'Constable Krumm is dead. He's been killed at the station.'

Eileen Baker was unsure of what had happened from that point in time.

After she finished giving evidence, the main witness for the police, Charles Yorke, was called. However, Yorke was not present. Major Yeldham asked why this was and was told by Daly that the witness did not wish to attend the inquiry. Major Yeldham said that regardless of his personal feelings on the matter Yorke would have to attend, as he was the only person who knew exactly what had happened in the station that night. Yeldham then told Daly to serve Yorke with a warrant if necessary. Daly informed the inquiry that Yorke had made a statement the day after the shooting, which was then read out before the inquiry:

> I am a chauffeur and a driver to Mr Walsh, of the Dunlop Rubber Co. I had known Constable Krumm for a few weeks. I met him last night at Baker's Hotel, and he was dressed in civilian clothes. I had never seen him in uniform, but I know he is a motor-driver in the R.I.C. He suggested my coming up to meet the mail train to get the evening paper – the train gets in about 12 midnight – and I did. There was a fair good crowd when we got there, including lots of youngish fellows. When we got the papers I started out from the platform reading it, and Krumm was close behind me. Just coming through the arch coming out, I heard a shot and then someone in front of me said, 'Hands up!' and put a revolver pointing towards me. I put up my hands. I saw Krumm struggling, and the man he was struggling with shouted for help. Two or three did come to his help. We heard a number of shots. I saw a revolver in the hand of one man as well as the man who held me up. My back was partly to Krumm. I saw Krumm fall and another man fall, too. I was searched and told to go away, and I went. I went to Baker's. I was followed up. All engaged were youngish – about 25.

Private Smyth of the Connaught Rangers was the garrison provost at the railway station on the night of the shootings and was called to give his evidence. He said that a few minutes after the train pulled in he heard a volley of shots. A woman and some children ran to him, pleading with him to save them.

He saw a man lying near the left side of the arch entrance. He was alive, but blood was pouring from him. A railway porter got a stretcher and four men removed the wounded man. He also said that he did not notice anything unusual before hearing the shots. Most of the crowd 'scattered' when the shots were fired. Daly then asked Smyth if he had seen anyone disorderly or under the influence of drink before the shots were fired.

Smyth replied, 'I did not.'

Another witness, Dr Fintan Campbell, the resident surgeon at the hospital, was also called. Although he was at the station at the time, he was not aware of the event that led to the shootings, but was called to attend a wounded man lying face down and covered in blood. There was nothing he could do at the scene, he said, so he ordered that the man be taken to the hospital and he ran ahead of the stretcher bearers. He said that the other man, Krumm, was dead when he went to attend him at the hospital: he had been shot in the head and there was no exit wound.

The only witness called in the Seamus Quirke case was Dr William Sands, who had attended the young man on the night he was killed. He told the inquest that he was called to the Burbidge home on Dock Road, where he found Quirke being attended by a priest. He said the man was dying from internal haemorrhaging caused by a number of bullet wounds. When asked if Quirke said anything before dying, Dr Sands replied, 'Not to me.' He was asked if there were any 'relatives' available who might be able to explain what had happened. Dr

Sands was unable to answer with certainty as young Quirke was from Cork and had no family in Galway.

In the case of Seán Mulvoy the only witnesses called were Doctors Campbell and Brereton and the head nurse. Dr Brereton stated that Mulvoy had been shot twice: one bullet struck him in the left leg below the knee and the other in the right side of the head. He said that there were no exit wounds and that Mulvoy died at about 3 a.m. Dr Campbell and the nurse corroborated Dr Brereton's evidence and added that the wounded man remained unconscious until he died. Major Yeldham asked if Seán Mulvoy's relatives had been notified about the inquiry. Daly replied that he didn't think that they would give evidence. Yeldham replied that they should have been given the opportunity to attend if they so wished, again asking Daly whether they had been notified. Daly replied, 'I do not know, Sir.' The inquest was then postponed to allow time for further witnesses to come forward. A direct order was also issued that Charles Yorke be contacted and attend the inquest when it resumed.

The inquiry resumed on Wednesday 15 September 1920, with Charles Yorke in attendance. He more or less told the same story as he had recorded in his statement. When he was asked why he did not go to the assistance of Constable Krumm, he reminded the inquiry that he was being held at gunpoint. When asked why he did not report the shootings at Eglinton Street RIC Barracks until the following morning, he replied that he was being 'shadowed' after leaving the station. Daly asked what he meant by 'shadowed', and Yorke replied that someone was following him. Because of this he decided that it would be safer to return to the hotel rather than go to the police. Another witness, Captain Canning from Salthill, was called to give evidence, but he had only arrived on the scene after the shots were fired, so had little to say regarding the matter.[12] According to Margetts, another witness who came forward was a girl who was known to be on very friendly terms with the Tans, and the information she gave proved to be a farce.[13] It was noted that the inquiry was open to the public and a request was issued for anyone who had witnessed the shooting to give evidence, but no one else came forward.

The following verdict was returned regarding Krumm: 'The court find [*sic*] that Constable Ed. Krumm died as a result of bullet wounds on September 9, 1920, and that the wounds were willfully inflected [*sic*] by some person or persons unknown.' A verdict on Seán Mulvoy and Seamus Quirke was deemed impossible because of a lack of evidence. Given that the Public Commission of Inquiry had been disrupted by the police and the military inquiry was being held in Renmore Barracks, it is not surprising that people did not come forward. There had also been a lot of raids and attacks on houses since the shootings and people were for the most part very frightened of reprisals, which suited the police and the Tans.[14]

12

Terror Stalks the Streets

Terror stalked the streets of Galway from this period until the signing of the Anglo-Irish Treaty. In the weeks following the shootings the Tans and Auxiliaries went on a rampage in the town. Houses were attacked and shots fired through the windows of dwellings. During curfew hours raids were carried out, mainly by masked and armed gunmen dressed as civilians. Houses were bombed and looted every night during September 1920. Businesses were targeted and in one shop alone £10,000 worth of damage was done.

One story was recorded of the window of a boot shop in the centre of the town being smashed by the Tans. The looters then sat calmly on the pavement, vainly trying on boots to find a pair that fitted. It took them some time to realise that there was only one boot from each pair on the window display. They left the pavement covered in footwear and walked away, cursing the Irish for 'doing things by halves'.[1]

The MacGettrick family's insurance business in Abbeygate Street was terrorised when the Tans and Auxiliaries burst through the front door, threatening the family with rifles.

After this attack, more property just around the corner in Mary Street was damaged by the same men. In Francis Street, they forced Harry Shields and his family out of their home, telling them to take their belongings and find shelter elsewhere as their house was to be used as a police depot. They also commandeered some twelve houses in Eyre Street, Henry Street and St John's Terrace. In almost all cases these were the homes of working men with families and they were given little time to remove their belongings.[2] On 22 September 1920, Thomas Nolan's Republican Outfitters business in High Street was attacked, the lock on the door shot open and the front window smashed. Most of Nolan's merchandise was thrown out on to the street; some of it was destroyed, while other items were stolen.[3]

While efforts were made by some British soldiers to prevent outrages, it became almost impossible to control the situation as it deteriorated into bloodshed. A number of raids were instigated by informers, far more, in fact, than was generally supposed. One of the worst aspects of this type of raid was that many of those denounced as republicans in reality had no connection with the movement. Much of this misinformation was driven by jealousy and spite, and was sometimes provided by so-called 'friends' of the victims. Fortunately, the army gave little credence to malicious gossip, being well aware of the situation. However, it was a very different story when 'half-intoxicated freebooters anxiously awaiting any excuse to raid, rob and loot' were given such information. They used it to their full advantage.[4]

Homes and businesses outside the town area and around the countryside were also targeted. In Salthill bullets were fired through the shop window of Joseph Grehan while a bomb was thrown through the back window. The Ballinasloe House (The Bal) was a regular target, as it was a well-known republican haunt. The Donnelly home in Barna was also attacked with bombs and bullets. The only occupants of the house at the time were Mrs Donnelly and her two terror-stricken daughters. That same night, Patrick Concanon from Barna was walking home after visiting his brother-in-law when he was stopped and physically and verbally abused by the Tans. They then told him to say his prayers while they fired their weapons close to him. The terrified man was then allowed to go home. Upon reaching Spiddal, the Tans attacked more houses and fired shots through the windows of other homes.[5]

A shocking incident that occurred near Loughrea in September was the terrorising of a young girl named Kathleen Lyons, who was pushed off her bicycle by soldiers while cycling to school in Loughrea. They enquired about her religion and the terrified girl replied that she was Catholic. One of them then said 'Shoot her!' which set the little girl screaming for her life. The child was in a state of terror and after a few moments one of the soldiers convinced the others to let her pass.[6]

Priests from the various parishes were calling for calm and also counselling people as best they could. At mass in the Abbey church the following Sunday, Fr Peter, OFM, asked the people to have patience for now, advising that things would change. He understood their fear and frustration with the authorities because of the absolute lawlessness of those controlling the town. He concluded with strong words of hope, saying, 'England's present reign of tyranny was unexampled, the darkest hour was before the dawn' and that Ireland was growing nearer to the 'glorious day of freedom'.[7]

On 27 September 1920, a lorry load of Auxiliaries arrived in Moycullen while Sunday mass was in progress. As the people left the church they were confronted by a large force of armed men. The men were separated from the women and taken to a nearby field while the women were allowed to return to their homes. The officer in charge then addressed the prisoners and told them that Richard Abbot, agent for the late Colonel Campbell, would be returning to Moycullen during the following week to take over the residence of Home Farm. He warned them that if Abbot was intimidated in any way, they would come back and the people of Moycullen would suffer as a consequence of this action. The men were then allowed to leave.[8]

Two weeks later the farm of Michael Walsh and his family, who lived near Moycullen, was surrounded by armed military and Tans. They proceeded to cause as much trouble as possible for the family, letting out the pigs and shooting the geese. They then entered the house to cause more destruction and following this the family – mother, father, sisters and brothers – were ordered into a field at gunpoint. They were then ordered out onto the road, where they were lined up against a wall and threatened with being shot. Shots were fired over their heads and one of the boys was wounded in the jaw. The family were beaten about the head and shoulders. Other homes were also raided that day, resulting in a number of men being savagely beaten and flogged.[9] Even people with permits to be out after curfew were harassed, as were people arriving on the late trains from Dublin.

A short time after the Krumm Inquiry, the girl who had given evidence in favour of the Tans was taken by masked men, who cut off her hair. The Tans retaliated by raiding the houses of IRA supporters and cutting off the hair of two girls.[10]

Another girl they singled out was Margaret 'Peg' Broderick, a sister of Seán Broderick, who was on the run at the time. Peg was noted for her good looks and long, beautiful hair, and was the envy of many young women at the time. She had joined Cumann na mBan in 1917 and later was appointed a section commander. Her duties included disrupting army recruiting meetings, observing RIC patrols and carrying dispatches, some to General Seán MacEoin. One duty she really hated to perform was enticing British soldiers to go down by the dock area, where IRA men were waiting to relieve them of their arms. She also visited prisoners in Galway Jail, bringing them parcels of food and other items on the pretence of being related to the prisoner. One British soldier became familiar with her and, suspecting something, once asked her, 'Are you a mother, an aunt or a sister today?' However, he always allowed her through.

Peg's first real run-in with the authorities was in Barna, where she and her companions, one being a Volunteer officer named Sheils, were challenged by the police. They continued walking through the village and as they passed the RIC barracks a sergeant and five or six policemen made an attempt to arrest Sheils. The women immediately pounced on the police, Peg jumping onto the back of one of the policemen and grabbing him by the throat. He had to release his hold on Sheils to try to free himself from her grip. Another policeman ran to his aid and pulled Peg off his colleague. As he did so, she grabbed his hat and proceeded to beat him with it. The other officer then turned and struck Peg with his revolver across the head, sending her reeling against the wall. She was stunned, and staggered, leaning on the wall for support. Someone shouted that this was no time to faint, which brought her somewhat to her senses. By this time, Sheils had been dragged into the barracks. Shots were fired over the women's heads by the police, who continually used vile language against their attackers. Peg and the others then grabbed stones from the ground around them and broke every window in the barracks before leaving.

Because of her open involvement with the republicans, Peg was known to the authorities. She was upstairs when the Tans arrived at her house and shouted down, requesting time to get dressed. They refused and ordered her to come down immediately. As she reached the bottom of the stairs, she grabbed her coat from the hall stand. The Tans held her family at gunpoint and as they pulled her out into the street she heard her mother shout, 'Be brave, Peg.' At that moment she believed that she was going to be shot, but one of them grabbed her by the hair and said, 'What wonderful curls you've got.' They held her securely and began to cut her hair down to the scalp with rough scissors. When they finished, they pushed her against the front door, simply said 'Goodnight' and walked away. It was a terrifying ordeal, but she remained calm. The following morning she had her head shaved so that her hair would grow again properly, and then went on the run. She never let her hair grow long again, keeping it short for the remainder of her life, some said to remind people of brutal times.[11]

On the evening of 16 September 1920, four men, Joseph Athy, Patrick Burke, Tom Burke and John Burke, left Oranmore on a horse and cart to go home to Maree. They had been working for the county council in Oranmore that day. When they were about a quarter of a mile from Oranmore a volley of shots was fired from behind bushes on the right side of the road. The men tried to drive the horse on and threw themselves to the bottom of the cart, but could not escape quickly enough. The shooting continued and Patrick Burke was hit behind the ear and the knee, while Athy received a leg wound and was shot through the stomach. They managed to control the frightened horse and drove to Ardfry House. The owner, Mr Burkett, went in search of a doctor, while a local nurse did what she could for the wounded men. It was late when Dr Foley from Ardrahan arrived; he sent the casualties to St Brides Home in Galway. Patrick Burke's wounds were not life-threatening and he recovered rather quickly. However, twenty-two-year-old Joseph Athy was fatally wounded and died the following day. One of the men said that during the ambush he saw a military figure close to the bushes where the shooting took place and later saw another seven men crossing the fields. They were all certain that the attack was carried out by crown forces.

The remains of Joseph Athy were removed from St Brides Home the following afternoon and taken to St Joseph's church, where his coffin was draped in the tricolour. The funeral mass took place the following day, Sunday, and four priests were in attendance, including Fr Michael Griffin and Fr O'Meehan, both of whom were associated with the republican movement. The main celebrant was Bishop of Galway Thomas O'Dea. During the ceremony, Fr Griffin called for prayers for all men who died for the Irish cause. After the mass, the mile-long funeral cortège made its way to Kilcaemon Cemetery, where Joseph Athy was laid to rest. During the funeral police and military preceded the mourners and dispersed a group of men, some of whom were Volunteers, although not in uniform, seizing their bicycles. They also arrested a local man, John Coppinger, who they said was carrying incriminating documents, and took him back to Galway in an army lorry. The military then fired shots into the air to disperse the crowds at the funeral.[12]

Another man from Maree, Patrick Cloonan, was also shot dead during the troubles. Both Cloonan and Athy are recorded on a memorial plaque located opposite the present Maree parish church.

***

Although some members of the local RIC had taken part in the various attacks and supported the Tans and Auxiliaries in their actions, others did not. While many Irishmen had already resigned from the force, more left after these attacks. In Carraroe, for instance, Constables Reilly and Callanan, both with fourteen years' service, resigned and were joined by Constable Sullivan, who had done two years' service. In Rosmuck, Constable Feeley resigned after ten years' service. The Tuam, Dunmore and Woodford areas were also experiencing a similar trend of men with long service leaving. It seems to have been the same throughout the country.[13] This was a worry for the authorities, who were losing the policemen with local knowledge.

In response, some members of the security forces tried to challenge reports of lawless behaviour in the county. On 31 September 1920, Tans and Auxiliaries arrived at the offices of the *Connacht Tribune* and demanded to see the editor. The Auxiliary officer commanding wished to make a statement in the newspaper with regard to the 'bad' publicity they were receiving. This action was instigated by alleged reports of Black and Tans stealing alcohol during a raid on P. J. Flaherty's pub near the docks a few days earlier. He said that the only damage done was that both the front and back doors were smashed during the raid. He stated that, as officer commanding during the raid, he resented reports that his men had looted the premises. It seems strange given the terror perpetrated on the public and the destruction of houses and businesses, that this man wished to deny allegations of stealing alcohol. It was really a propaganda stunt in a bid to gain some good press.

The officer also included a statement from the Press Association to be published with his own report. It is interesting in that it records the wages earned by his men, as well as recruiting numbers:

We are called the Black and Tans and a great deal of misrepresentation and exaggeration has got abroad regarding us and our purpose here. The Black and Tans are really noncoms who have joined the R.I.C. proper; we are the Auxiliary force, and act independently. All our men are ex-officers, and, I hope, gentlemen. I wish it to be distinctly understood that we are not here to shoot people but to restore order. We are obliged to take certain steps to do this. The police are practically confined to their barracks and could not walk abroad in certain districts until we came. Peaceable, law-abiding citizens have nothing to fear from us.

The Press Association says: The Black and Tans, so called because of their hybrid uniform of green and khaki, were recruited solely on account of the shortage of men in Ireland. They are, it is stated, genuine recruits to the Royal Irish Constabulary, and it is only due to the lack of Royal Irish Constabulary uniforms that they appear in their present dress. The suggestion that these men are connected with the military was denied at the Irish Office. The Auxiliary division of the Royal Irish Constabulary, and named the Black and Tans on account of their uniforms, were recruited for the purpose of instructing the existing men of the original Royal Irish Constabulary in the defence of their barracks. These men are classed as cadets, given the rank of Sergeant, and paid at a rate of £1 a day. All of them are ex-officers and are a distinct section of the Black and Tans. The following figures supplied to the

Press Association indicate the present proportion of recruits: During the week ending September 19 there were 64 recruits of whom 61 came from Great Britain and three from Ireland. During the same period there were 96 recruits for the Auxiliary division (ex-officers) bringing the strength of the division up to over 500. Since then it has been further added to. The strength of the Royal Irish Constabulary is just under 10,000.[14]

13

Extended Tan Raids

In the early hours of Sunday 26 September 1920, four lorry loads of Black and Tans arrived in the village of Ardrahan. They immediately singled out a number of houses and set them on fire, giving the occupants just enough time to vacate their homes. The first house they targeted was that of a widow named Joyce and her young son, but they soon realised that they had the wrong house. It was the home of Patrick Joyce they had intended to attack. Once they identified his home, they smashed the windows and door, and upon entering demanded to know where his son John was hiding. Joyce told them that he had no idea where his son was at present. He was then ordered out of the house along with his younger son, Patrick. They were forced to stand against a wall while the Tans spread petrol throughout the house, then threw a bomb into the building, which set the whole house alight when it exploded. Joyce and his son were ordered to run up and down along the village road in just their nightshirts. There was no escape: the Tans seemed to be everywhere. They also fired shots through the door of Martin Kelly's house in Ardrahan, just missing Mrs Kelly, who was carrying a baby in her arms at the time.

After the Joyce house was gutted, the Tans drove to Labane, about a mile from Ardrahan, where they called to the home of John Burns, a national schoolteacher. Burns, his wife and four young children had already retired for the night and were asleep, but were awakened by the sudden loud hammering on the front door. Once the Tans gained entry, the frightened family, dressed only in nightshirts, were forced outside and ordered to run up and down the road.

The Tans then turned their attention to the Parochial Hall. Taking some hay from a local farmyard, they spread it in the hall, doused it with petrol and set it alight. The parish priest, Fr Carr, stated that he was awakened by a loud explosion at about 12.30 a.m., and 'Looking out of my bedroom window, I saw our beautiful parochial hall – an architectural gem – in flames. As bomb succeeded bomb, I could hear shouts that one could only expect in hell. It did not take long till the whole building was completely gutted.'

The homes of Michael Burke and John MacInerney were also targeted. The Tans first surrounded Burke's home, then burst into the house, dragged him and his two sons out onto the road, shoved them against an outside wall and told them they were going to be shot. The younger boy, who suffered from health problems, collapsed onto the ground. His brother and father knelt over him, trying to revive him. The family believed that this was possibly the reason their lives were spared, because the Tans then concentrated their efforts on burning the house. The family members were not given any time to save their possessions. All were dressed in the only clothes they now possessed, which were mainly nightshirts, and were forced at gunpoint to watch their home being destroyed. The Tans also torched the barns, outhouses and haggard, leaving absolutely nothing but devastation behind them. There was nothing anyone could do to stop the destruction, as the Tans were heavily armed and were shooting wildly into the houses, just waiting for someone to resist.

They then attacked the home of John MacInerney, whose brother Michael and his family were also living there. Both families were pulled out of the house and John and Michael were forced to stand against pillars leading into the garden. They were questioned at gunpoint as to the whereabouts of their brother Thomas (who also lived there, but was not at home that night). The brothers replied by saying that they had no idea where he was and that they had not seen him for some time. The Tans were annoyed and told them that they had only a few minutes to live. John asked them for time to pray before dying, to which one of the Tans replied, 'Little time yourselves would give,' and hit him in the face with his gun. John was given time to pray, but after several minutes noticed that the Tans were occupied watching the people who were gathering around the house. He took the opportunity to make his escape and ran down the garden, past the burning house and into the darkened fields behind the building. Shots rang out, but they missed, and he got away. The Tans did not follow John into the darkness – they had other prisoners. One of the officers then ordered his men not to shoot anyone unless he or she resisted. He added that a lot of damage had been done, but there was more to do before the night was over.

The home of John Higgins, his wife and their ten children was then targeted. Tans hammered on the door of the house until Higgins answered. Then, at gunpoint, they forced him into the kitchen, where one of them hit him in the back with the butt of a rifle. Higgins was asked how many sons he had and their ages, to which he replied that the children were all between two and fifteen years of age – none of them were old enough to be involved in politics. The Tans then went to the bedrooms and pulled the boys out of bed. All of them were ordered out of the house into the garden, where there were four stacks of barley. The Tans set the barley alight. Higgins asked them not to burn the house, but his plea fell on deaf ears, as they set fire to the corner of the building before leaving. After they left, the family managed to put out the fire, thus preventing the house from being destroyed. Like the others who had lost their homes and winter feed that night, the barley was all the Higgins family had to live on for the winter.

The flames over the village area could be seen for miles and many people fled their homes as word spread of the night of terror. It was reported that the only object that survived without damage from the burned houses that night was rosary beads, which gave people hope, as they believed that it was a sign that change was coming. Fr Carr called for restraint during mass the following week, and spoke of the brutality and criminal activity of the so-called authorities. In conclusion, he stated:

> If we are thus to follow in the footsteps of Our Divine Master and beg the intercession of His Holy Mother, we can rest assured, that though our poor country may have to suffer for a short time, her houses maybe razed to the ground, her sons imprisoned or put to death, still there is one thing that England cannot do and that is she cannot burn the grass of this Emerald Isle and from this soil of Ireland will arise a God-fearing, self-reliant people who will forgive, but cannot forget the savage acts perpetrated in the name of government.[1]

The attacks in Ardrahan seem to have pioneered a new way of targeting other areas of County Galway. Less than a month later, a group of Auxiliaries arrived in John Raftery's public house in Corofin, near Tuam. They had a number of drinks, paid for them and left. There was an air of anxiety while they were in the pub, so people were happy to see them leave. However, later that night they returned with a group of Tans, taking John Raftery at gunpoint to a location about a mile from his home and forcing him to crawl on his hands and knees for about thirty yards while being whipped across the back and legs with a leather belt. After the beating they pulled him up and made him face two men with revolvers pointed at his head. Four shots were fired over his shoulder, so close that Raftery received powder burns on the side of his face. He was then allowed to go free.

That same evening the men arrived at the home of the

Feeney family in Anbally, Cummer. The family was saying the rosary at the time of the attack. The four sons, Thomas, Martin, Willie and Paddy, were dragged out of the house while guns were held on the other members of the family. The four boys were stripped and flogged. A rope was tied around Thomas Feeney and he was pulled over a stone wall. One of the brothers attempted to help him and was knocked senseless with a blow across the head from a revolver. Before leaving, the military warned the boys that they were being watched.

A short time later the two lorries of Auxiliaries and Tans stopped at Varden's public house, also in Cummer. A group of men was there at the time, and they were surrounded by the British forces and asked if they were members of the republican police. No one responded. One man, Michael Welby, who attempted to escape, was shot in the back. The bullet passed through him. Although severely wounded, he managed to reach his home, where he collapsed before his shocked family. A doctor was then summoned. Meanwhile, back at Varden's pub the other men were stripped and flogged with leather straps, sticks and rifle butts. Shots were also fired over their heads in a bid to terrify them. A number of the men were severely injured and all of them had their clothing torn to shreds. The Auxiliaries and Tans then entered the pub, where they singled out a man named Michael Dolly, giving him a severe beating before leaving. As the lorries drove away a number of shots were fired at neighbouring houses, one bullet striking a girl named Nora Glynn in the leg as she ran to her front door. Another shot killed a dog.[2]

During October 1920 attacks by Auxiliaries and Tans also took place in Barna and Oranmore. In Barna, they forced their way into the bar and grocery premises of the O'Donnghailes, searched the house and held the family at gunpoint. Before leaving, they gave them a note stating, 'If you don't put your name in English in two days you will be shot – R.I.P.' In the Maree–Oranmore area, the band hall was burned down the following night. The farmhouse of the Devaney family was also targeted. The family were all in bed asleep when they were awakened by a loud knocking on the front door. After being admitted to the house, the Tans forced three of the brothers, Thomas, Stephen and Pat, out of the house. After questioning them for a few minutes, they were told to kneel down and pray, as they were going to be shot. Moments later they were told to get up, marched down the road and were halted some distance from the house. Shots were fired over their heads at first and then the three brothers were fired on with shotguns, all three of them being hit with around sixty pellets each, mainly in the legs, but also in the stomach. Inside the house, the terrified family was unable to do anything to help the boys. When their father tried, he was hit on the head with a revolver. The three brothers were taken to hospital in Galway that night. All of them made a full recovery.

The home of Joseph Athy was also targeted that night and his two brothers were taken out, marched along the road and warned about involvement in the republican movement.[3]

The IRA hit back at these attacks. On 30 October 1920 a party of five policemen who were making their way from

Peterswell to Kilchreest were ambushed by republicans at Castledaly. Constable Timothy Horan was wounded and made his way over a nearby cemetery wall. One of the republicans followed and shot him dead. One of Horan's colleagues, Constable Keane, was severely wounded in the attack. Following the ambush, the attackers took the policemen's weapons and equipment.[4]

Two days later, on 1 November 1920, Eileen Quinn from Kiltartan, Gort, was shot dead by Black and Tans, police or Auxiliaries as they passed her home in a lorry. The twenty-three-year-old married woman was sitting on a stile at the front of her house with her nine-month-old baby in her arms when a speeding military lorry passed. Shots were discharged from the back, one hitting Eileen in the abdomen. She managed to stagger back to the front door of her house, where a servant girl had come out to investigate what had happened. Handing the unharmed baby over to the girl, Eileen Quinn then collapsed, bleeding profusely and obviously in a lot of pain.[5] Fr John Considine, CC, Gort, was called to the scene and gave a graphic description of her last moments:

> It is too awful, too inhuman, to contemplate … I often felt my blood boil and I often prayed that the good God might change the minds and hearts of those cruel monsters. Little did I then dream that I should witness a tragedy, an atrocity more hideous, more revolting, more frightful, more brutal, more cruel … here in our own little peaceful parish of Gort. My God, it is awful! About three o'clock on Tuesday Malachy Quinn weeping bitterly, called for me. 'Father,' said he, 'I have just heard that my

wife has been shot. Will you run down immediately.' I procured a motor car and hurried to the scene. At the gateway there we beheld a large pool of blood. In the yard another pool, and the porch leading to the kitchen was covered with blood. I entered the room. Oh, God! what a sight. There lay the poor woman, the blood oozing out through her clothes. She turned her eyes towards me and said: 'Oh, Father John, I have been shot.' 'Shot!' I exclaimed. 'Yes,' she replied. By whom, I asked. 'Police,' she answered. 'By police!' 'Yes,' she replied emphatically. 'Did you see them?' 'Yes.' 'Where?' 'On a lorry.' 'How many lorries?' 'Two.' 'From what lorry did the shot come?' 'From the first.' She then became weaker, Father Considine explained, and on rallying exclaimed, 'Father John, will you do something for me?' I tried to console her, he explained, and administered the Last Sacrament. When I finished she whispered to me, 'Bring me Malachy, bring him to me, I hear him crying. I have something to tell him.' I did so. What a scene. Then she became weak and fainted off. Gradually she became worse. From 3 o'clock to 10.30 she lingered on in pain. Occasionally she would clasp my hand pull me towards her, and say: 'I'm done, I'm done!' At 10.30 her condition became worse, and we knelt by her bedside to recite the Rosary and prayers for the Dying. She tried to join, but was too weak. At 10.45 the little children began to cry, and with them the crowded house burst into tears. As I read the last prayer of the Ritual she looked around, then closed her eyes and died. My God![6]

This was a double tragedy for the family, as Eileen was seven months pregnant at the time. Her three surviving children were all under four years of age.

This appalling murder of an innocent woman and her

unborn baby sent shockwaves throughout the county.[7] The murder was raised in the House of Commons and a military inquiry followed. One of the police stated that he did hear shots being fired from the vehicle he was driving, but said that he did not see any woman. He also said that when travelling along a suspicious-looking place like a wood the men would often fire their rifles in the air, but not near a house or near a 'decent-looking civilian'. He claimed he did not hear of a woman having been shot until he got to Galway. He added that he did not notice a woman on the wall between Gort and Ardrahan. After all the evidence was given, which was mainly from the police, the verdict of the military inquiry was announced as follows:

> The court having considered the evidence and the medical evidence are of opinion that Mrs Eileen Quinn, of Corker, Gort in the county of Galway, met her death due to shock and haemorrhage by a bullet wound in the groin fired by some occupant of a police car proceeding along the Gort–Ardrahan road on the 1st November, 1920. They are of the opinion that the shot was one of the shots fired as a precautionary measure and in view of the facts record a verdict of death by misadventure.[8]

14

Singled Out for Murder

The month of October had opened with the shooting of Sinn Féin activist and secretary of the local Sinn Féin club John O'Hanlon. On the night of Saturday 2 October 1920, O'Hanlon was at home on the Lackagh Road near Knockdoe with his father and mother. His wife, Mary, and their two children – a three-year-old girl, Maureen, and a nine-month-old baby, William – were also in the house. It was about 11 p.m. and everything seemed normal. The family was sitting having supper and John was polishing his boots for Sunday mass when there was a heavy knock on the front door and a call demanding entry to the house. John said goodbye to his family, telling them that he would contact them as soon as it was safe to do so, and then made his way out the back door.

The Tans and Auxiliaries had made their way from Turloughmore to O'Hanlon's home, stopping a few hundred yards away near a little bridge. Some of them had disembarked from the truck, made their way through the fields and surrounded the back entrance to the house. They waited, guns ready, in the darkness of the cold autumn night. Once they were in position, their comrades continued along the road until they arrived at the front door, where they stopped, and two armed officers knocked loudly and demanded entry. John's father opened the door to the two armed men, one dressed in a long black coat and the other wearing a trench coat. There were about fourteen other uniformed men in the garden at this stage. The two officers entered the house and began a search. It was while they were carrying out this inspection that two gunshots were heard from the back of the house. John O'Hanlon had been making his way across the backyard to a small apple garden. His escape route took him over a stile in the stone wall. As he crossed over the wall, the Tans waiting in the darkness opened fire, killing him instantly. They left his body where it fell.

In the house the family members were being held in the main room. When John was not to be found, they were questioned. John's father was asked why his son had run away and where he was running to. While they had all heard the gunshots that had killed John, the family assumed that he must have escaped, otherwise why were the Tans still asking about him?

After the Tans left, William O'Hanlon went outside to investigate, but although his son lay dead only yards away, he didn't find him in the darkness. John's wife, Mary, believed that he had gone to a safe house. This had been a frightening night; one which they were all delighted was over as they retired. It never entered their heads that John had been shot.

The following morning, Mary got up early to prepare breakfast for the children and dress them for mass. She made her way to the kitchen and while going about her morning duties she looked out of the back window. To her horror, the lifeless body of her young husband was lying across the stile. Panic set in immediately and she called for help. The family was heartbroken, shocked and horrified to think that John had been killed so callously and left to die alone so close to his home, while they had been cold-heartedly questioned regarding his whereabouts by men who probably realised that he was already dead.

Concerned neighbours began arriving to help support the family. The kitchen was cleared and became a makeshift funeral parlour as the body was laid on the table. The local priest arrived and made funeral arrangements for the following day. However, the times had to be changed so that friends could attend without being confronted by the Tans and Auxiliaries, who were keeping a close watch on proceedings. It seems that a policeman came to the house that morning and informed the family that the Tans would possibly disrupt the funeral. The mass had been arranged for 3 p.m. in Lackagh church, but because of the warning it was decided to hold the ceremony an hour earlier, in the hope that the funeral would be over before the Tans arrived. The requiem mass was celebrated by Fr John O'Malley, PP, and during the service he condemned the cold-blooded murder. Following the mass, John's remains were taken to Lackagh Old Cemetery a few hundred yards from his home for burial.[1] Just as the policeman had warned, the Tans and Auxiliaries arrived and began firing shots over the heads of the mourners. They physically attacked some of the people as they made their way home and according to one report raided the O'Hanlons' house again, this time ransacking it. They also raided Flynn's pub in Lackagh, forcing those on the premises outside at gunpoint, then ordering them to run as shots rang out.[2]

An incident reported in the *Dublin Evening Mail* on 28 June 1920, four months earlier, may provide a possible motive for the murder of John O'Hanlon. It stated that five policemen were surrounded by fifteen armed men in Lackagh village and had their bicycles and capes taken before being allowed to return to Turloughmore. The official inquiry into John O'Hanlon's death stated that he was 'Shot by armed forces of the Crown when failing to halt when challenged to do so three times by Armed forces of the Crown.' The people expected no other verdict, as it was normal practice for the Tans to shoot someone and say that he had been trying to escape. There is no doubt that John O'Hanlon was singled out and murdered because he believed in Irish freedom and was prepared to stand up for his beliefs.[3]

Willie Cullinane was another man from the parish of Lackagh to be killed. After leaving school, he had gone on to study for the priesthood in All Hallows College, Dublin. A keen follower of Gaelic games, he had been attending the match in Croke Park on 21 November 1920 when the Black and Tans attacked the stadium. He managed to get out of the park, but was shot by the Tans as he made his way back to the college. He was laid to rest in Lackagh Cemetery.[4]

On 4 October 1920, a dance was disrupted at Knockroon near Headford by Auxiliaries and five men were singled out. Their female companions were told to go home, after which the men were flogged. Some of them were also struck with rifle butts. Houses in Headford were also raided that night. It seems that these raids were carried out by Scottish regiments. During one of the raids, they banged on the front door of Patrick Cullen, an RIC constable who was considering resigning from the force, and dragged him onto the road in his nightshirt. He was flogged with sticks and a leather strap and branded a traitor. They then threw him over a wall and went back to search the house, terrifying his wife even more. Cullen was taken to a local doctor, who described the victim as being a 'mass of discoloured flesh'.[5]

On 21 October 1920, mass was disrupted in Strawberryhill, near Dunmore, by an armed soldier who went up to the altar and ordered everyone out of the church. The priest, Fr Macken, confronted the soldier and told him that no one was leaving the church until mass was over. The soldier then left the church and joined his comrades outside. Upon leaving mass, the people were challenged by an officer and seven soldiers. They said that they were investigating the hold-up of a mail car some days earlier. Fr Macken again defended the people and told the officer that he was making a mistake. He also said that such outrageous conduct in a church was unknown in any civilised country. The officer warned the congregation that if another mail car was held up in the area, the soldiers would be back to burn their houses. The soldiers then made their way to Dunmore where they conducted a search of the cemetery for arms.[6]

That night in Gurraun, Oranmore, the military arrived at the home of Roger Furey and his two sons and demanded entry to the house. Once allowed in, they brought the two young men outside and forced them to stand against the barn wall, asking them if they knew anything about the Merlin Park ambush earlier that year. When the boys denied any knowledge of the attack, they were told to kneel down and say their prayers as they were going to be shot. The Tans forced the barrel of the gun into the mouth of one of the young men, Michael, while another Tan shot him in the leg. He was then shot across the ear with the revolver. The officer commanding then ordered his men to set the brothers free. A short time later the Tans raided the home of Thomas Furey and his sons, John, Stephen and Tom, cousins of Roger Furey's sons. They received similar treatment, John being wounded in the arm. Their next stop was the home of Martin King near Oranmore, where they smashed all the windows and beat his sons, Martin and Paddy, also wounding their father in the attack.[7]

On Sunday 24 October 1920, at about 10.30 p.m., four policemen knocked on the door of Egan's bar and grocery shop in Coshla. The owner, Thomas Egan, was in the kitchen taking off his boots and preparing for bed. His wife, who had been putting the children to bed at the time, went to open the door. The police sergeant asked who else was in the house and she told him just her husband and children. He then asked to see the premises, so she took the four men through the shop and into the kitchen. There was a small doorway in the hall leading to a storeroom, and they asked to see this room also. They then continued through to the kitchen. As they entered, Thomas Egan stood up, and the police officer asked Mrs Egan about the identity of the man. She replied that he was her husband. One of the policemen rushed at him and knocked him against the kitchen press. He was then grabbed by the back of the neck and had his head knocked against the press. As Egan bent down to pick up his cap, the other policemen rushed him, trying to force him out of the house. Mrs Egan tried to get between the police and her husband, but the sergeant shot him twice with a revolver over her shoulder. Egan fell to the ground and as he lay there another policeman shot him again, this time with a double-barrelled shotgun. The gunshot covered Mrs Egan with powder. The shots had woken the children, who ran to their mother. Mrs Egan called out to the Sacred Heart of Jesus for protection. When she saw the blood on her husband's face, she shouted out to the children that their father had been shot. One of the policemen began mimicking the distressed woman's crying. The policeman with the shotgun shoved the barrel of the weapon up to her mouth, threatening to kill her before leaving.

The men then left, firing their weapons into the night. Afterwards, Mrs Egan helped her husband sit up against the kitchen wall and said an Act of Contrition for him. He opened his eyes and looked at her, but was unable to speak. He died about twenty minutes later. The police had made no attempt to question Thomas Egan – like John O'Hanlon, it seems he was singled out for murder. Although some people later suggested that Egan had been questioned about the shooting of Shawe-Taylor some months earlier, close to his pub, Mrs Egan stated that this was not true. He had been questioned about the killing at the time, but so had almost every man in the district.

Neighbours began arriving soon afterwards to support and comfort the distressed Egan family. Thomas Egan was laid out on the kitchen table of his home. The family was not allowed to remove the remains until a military inquiry was completed. During the inquest which followed, Mrs Egan was asked if she recognised any of the policemen involved, but she said that she had never seen them before. The judge also asked her if any policeman had called to the house prior to the incident. She told the court that a policeman had visited them on Sunday afternoon, but he was an old friend of the family and would not have played any role in the killing of her husband. Her husband, she attested, never took an interest or part in politics, and stated that all who knew him found it strange that he had been attacked. When summing up, the court gave permission for the burial to take place, but ordered that no more than fifty people could attend.[8]

15

Murder at Long Walk

On 22 September 1920 at least twelve men, some uniformed Black and Tans, burst into the Old Malt House pub and grocery business in High Street. The proprietor was Michael Walsh, a Sinn Féin councillor and officer in the IRA. He was a native of Headford, but by this period was living in Galway city. With his wife Agnes, he had eight children ranging in age from two to twelve years old. It was about 1.30 a.m. when the Tans arrived. After breaking down the door, they rushed upstairs to where Agnes Walsh and her children were sleeping and demanded to know the whereabouts of her husband. Agnes told them that she didn't know. They then searched the entire building, firing shots and exploding grenades, causing extensive damage to the property. They shot open the safe and removed its contents, as well as stealing money from the till in the bar. The terrified woman and her children remained upstairs, afraid to move. Other items stolen included clothing, cigarettes, tobacco, various grocery items, beer and stout. The men then turned on the bar taps, emptying the barrels of their contents. Before leaving, they smashed doors, cabinets and other items of furniture. The damage was later estimated at £1,000.[1]

The head constable in Eglinton Street Barracks, Daniel Lyons, had secretly warned Michael Walsh that his life was in danger.[2] Being a member of Galway Urban Council and trying to run a business, Walsh was in a rather difficult position. If he went on the run, the authorities would definitely know that he was connected to the IRA; however, by staying, he was also exposing himself to danger. Although it was obvious that the Tans would return to seek him out, being a courageous man, Michael Walsh opted to stay and face whatever his fate might be.

One evening brothers Michael and Sweeney Newell were in the pub. The purpose of their visit is unknown. Upon leaving, they were challenged by a number of armed Black and Tans. The Newells were determined not to be taken away for interrogation and attacked the Tans before they had a chance to use their guns. A fight ensued, and a sailor in full Royal Navy uniform became involved in the fight and began punching and disarming the Tans. He was a powerful man and his attack was so volatile that the Tans panicked and ran from the scene, leaving their weapons behind. While there was little time for making acquaintances, the brothers shook the sailor's hand and thanked him, before grabbing the discarded weapons and making their way back to Castlegar. A search of Galway and the docks was conducted the following day in a bid to find the sailor, but his ship had left port early that morning, so he escaped detection. However, people speculated as to who the mysterious sailor who had come to the aid of the republicans had been. Commenting on the fight many years later, Sweeney Newell said that the sailor was the strongest man he had ever seen, and that he most definitely saved them from a severe beating or even death that night, adding that he believed the sailor to have been Jimmy Philbin from Bohermore, a Royal Navy champion boxer.[3]

Almost a month after the first raid, the Tans raided the Old Malt House again, on Tuesday 19 October 1920. It was about 10 p.m. when five Tans arrived, dressed as civilians but armed with revolvers. They entered the premises, ordered the people who were in the bar to leave and told a seventeen-year-old shop assistant, Martin Meenaghan, to remove the light bulb from the inner bar. They then took all the cash from the till and the safe, which was still broken from the previous raid. Cigarettes and tobacco were again targeted, and one raider even stuffed a box of OXO cubes into his pocket. Another held Michael Walsh and young Meenaghan prisoner at gunpoint, while the others proceeded to search the premises. Walsh asked Meenaghan to pour him a whiskey while he was waiting. The nearest drink at hand was rum, so he gave him a glass of that instead. However, before Walsh could drink it, one of the Tans said that the drink would only be wasted, adding, 'You'll be dead within the hour.' Walsh replied that if this were the case he would like to see a priest, but the Tan refused, adding that priests were 'worse than yourselves' and that Walsh had 'shot a lot of police'. Walsh denied this, adding that he was not aware of police being shot in Galway, but his accuser retorted that they had been shot outside Galway. The other Tans returned, pointed their revolvers at the prisoners and asked Walsh if Meenaghan was his son. Walsh replied that he was not, that the boy was an apprentice.

Looking at Meenaghan, the leader then asked, 'Are you a rebel?' Young Meenaghan replied, 'I am,' and was then told that he would 'get the same' as Walsh. Four of the Tans took Walsh outside into the street, barely giving him a chance to grab his hat, while one of them remained in the pub guarding Meenaghan.

After the others had left the Old Malt House, Meenaghan asked the Tan who was guarding him, 'Are you going to shoot me?' The Tan answered by saying that they knew nothing about him, so for now he was not in danger of being shot. He also told Meenaghan that they were all members of the English secret service and that they knew who they were targeting.

At about 10.20 p.m. Walsh was ordered to walk down towards Quay Street.[4] As he reached Cross Street, there was a group of men standing at the corner. These men later stated that two of the Tans walked ahead of Michael Walsh while the other two walked either side of him, and all had guns drawn. One of the men at the corner was Martin Flaherty from Henry Street, who knew Walsh and was the last person to speak to him, saying, 'Good night, Michael.' Michael responded, 'Good night, Martin.'[5] As Walsh and his captors reached the end of Quay Street, it appears that Walsh asked where they were taking him, but the Tans simply pushed him towards the Spanish Arch. According to a report by someone who was in the area that night, one of the Tans said to Walsh that he was going to 'meet his maker', but this is unsubstantiated. The group passed under the Spanish Arch and continued along an area known as Long Walk, with a row of houses on one side and on the other a quay, where the river runs into the sea. A little over halfway along this road, the Tans shot Walsh through the head and dumped his body into the sea. They then returned quickly to the pub. It was about 10.45 p.m. when they re-entered the premises, looking flushed. All five then muttered together in the kitchen. As they left, one of them took Michael Walsh's overcoat. They told Meenaghan to get back to his lodgings and warned him that if he told anyone what had taken place he would be shot within twenty-four hours.

Agnes Walsh was aware that something was wrong and was trying to protect her children; however, a short time later she went to investigate. When she was informed by neighbours that her husband had been taken in the direction of the docks, she feared the worst. She went to the Augustinian church in Middle Street to request help from Fr Duffy, who immediately went to seek information. Early the following morning a number of men who were on their way to work noticed a man's hat on the riverbank. On closer examination it was found to be bloodstained, and there were also two large pools of blood found close to the quay. Looking into the tidal river, they were horrified to see a body in about ten feet of water. At about 9 a.m. Michael Walsh's body was removed from the river and taken to his home amid scenes of shock and grief. The hair on one side of his head was clotted with blood, and there was a finger-sized jagged bullet wound in his temple and an exit wound on the opposite side of his head. An empty cartridge was found close to the scene of the murder. Although Dr Kinkead, who examined the body, stated that one bullet had been used and that death was instantaneous, residents of Long Walk said that they had heard two shots at about 10.20 the previous night. The district inspector of police arrived at the Walsh home and informed the family that the body could not be removed for burial until a military investigation had taken place. However, the following day permission was given to take the remains to church. At 6 p.m. that evening, the body of Michael Walsh was taken to the Pro-Cathedral in Middle Street, a strong military and police presence lining the route.

The funeral took place the following morning after 11 a.m. mass, and was limited to the clergy and fifty people, including relatives. Eighteen priests concelebrated the mass, among them Fr Michael Griffin, who would suffer a similar fate some three weeks later. All business premises in the town closed during the funeral and the streets were lined with people. Motorists were stopped at checkpoints coming into the town and were questioned and had their papers checked – they had been warned to carry identification. Both the military and police were on duty at the Pro-Cathedral and along the route to the New Cemetery. The Dragoon Guards, with sabres drawn, were also on duty at various locations. When the remains were removed for burial, a number of priests led the way, with Michael Walsh's family and friends walking behind the hearse. The poignancy was heightened by the children taking their places ahead of the adult mourners. The military and police placed themselves between the mourners and the huge crowds of people following the funeral. An armoured car also followed the procession. Crowds thronged the footpaths in order to pay their respects. When the funeral cortège reached Eyre Square, a cordon of military, Tans, Auxiliaries and police were drawn across the street and the people were ordered to return to their homes. This order was followed by a detachment of cavalry patrolling the town.

Among the floral tributes to Michael Walsh was a wreath with a note from a cousin, Fr Murphy, which read, 'Joy, not tears. He died for Ireland.'[6] It was rumoured at the time that Walsh had been brought to the attention of the authorities by Joseph Young, another member of Galway Urban Council, a unionist, and a senior member of the Galway Recruiting Committee during the Great War. It was believed that there were serious differences of opinion between the two men. One of the Tans involved was a man named Miller; the others were not identified. In recent years a memorial plaque was unveiled at Long Walk in memory of Michael Walsh.

On 23 October 1920, Whelan's pub (Stage Door) in Woodquay, along with some other private houses, was raided. The Tans demanded that the residents hand over the contents of their safes. Whelan's pub was the last premises to be raided that night. Although it was raining, Mrs Whelan was ordered outside in her nightclothes. She ran to a relative, Luke Walsh, who lived in the area. Meanwhile, one of the Tans, knowing that there was a young woman who worked in the pub upstairs at the time, rushed in to find her, but she jumped from a back room window, also in her nightclothes, and fled to the safety of a nearby house.[7]

Raids in the city continued. Galway was under siege by the very forces that, according to the British government, had been sent there to restore order. A number of attacks took place in the city during the night of 26 October 1920. In Dominick Street, the shop and post office of the Brown family was set alight; it had already been targeted a number of times. Mrs Brown was alone in the shop at the time. She was lucky that neighbours heard the shattering of the glass in the front of the building and her screams for help, and were able to rescue her from the burning building. A pub known as Ward's in Cross Street was also attacked because of a sign in Gaelic over the door. The Tans took Mrs Ward out into the street and told her to have the sign removed or they would destroy the place. She explained that the sign, which read 'Naughton', was simply her first husband's name: she had been married twice. The Tans then asked who was in the house with her and she replied that there was only her seventeen-year-old son, Patrick Naughton. They then went upstairs and brought the teenager down to the street, two of the military pointing revolvers at his head, and gave her twenty-four hours to remove the sign or they would shoot the boy.

The next attack took place a short time later in Sea Road,

when a grenade was thrown through the fanlight window of Sammons' shop.[8] There were attacks on Moylett's grocery and general wholesale and retail businesses in Williamsgate Street on two consecutive nights. The Tans or Auxiliaries, or both, were again responsible. On the first night they simply broke through the front window and made away with some foodstuffs and other commodities. The second night they blew open the safe and took the entire contents of £160, and again helped themselves to any goods they deemed useful. The police were called the following morning, but said that they had no idea about who might be responsible. That same week, a number of businesses in the town were searched, including O'Gorman and Company, Brennan's drapery, Naughton's merchant business and Slator printers. The railway station was also being watched and train drivers, firemen and guards were searched upon arrival in Galway.

16

Intelligence Operations

While all these attacks were going on the IRA was not idle. Important work was going on to establish legitimate targets and opportunities for attack. As previously mentioned, Tom Courtney was involved in checking letters passing through the post office in Galway for the IRA. Another post office man involved in this operation was Joe Togher, who had been born on 8 September 1898 in Headford, where his father was a shopkeeper. He had three brothers and one sister, all of whom were still children when their father died. The family moved into Galway when Joe was very young, and he attended the old 'Mon' national school in Lombard Street. He began working in the post office in 1915 and a short time later joined the Irish Volunteers in Castlegar. By 1919 he was working in the sorting office, a position that was to prove vital to the republican movement, where he copied mails he suspected were useful to the movement and deciphered coded letters. He later stated in his witness statement:

I dealt personally with all the incoming and outgoing mails for both the military and R.I.C. at Renmore Barracks and Eglinton Barracks. It meant quite a lot of night work for me in order to ensure no delay. To enter the office at night, which I could not do officially, I was obliged to climb through a second floor window, extract any mail I was doubtful about, bring them back home, break up the cipher and pass the information to the Brigade Commandant, Seamus Murphy.

This worked well for a time, until Togher ran into a problem with a telegram and had to take it with him rather than copying the details. This resulted in all telegrams being locked away at night. However, he managed to make a replica of the key and was soon back in business.

By October 1920 a serious effort was being made by the IRA to identify informers. The East Connemara Company knew that someone was giving information to the authorities about the Barna and Moycullen areas. It was clear that the Tans had precise information on which houses to target and the locations where drilling and training were taking place. A Volunteer named John Hosty, who had pioneered the IRA secret service, approached Joe Togher and asked for his help in trying to identify who was leaking information to the police. In the weeks that followed, Togher intercepted five letters addressed to the County Office of the Black and Tans in Eglinton Street Barracks, the OC Military Station at Earls Island and the OC in Renmore Barracks. They were all addressed in the same handwriting and signed 'A Friend',[1] but one letter also carried the signature P. W. Joyce.[2] It was obvious from the contents that it was this man who was passing on the information. Togher took the letters to the Connemara Brigade commander, Commandant Michael Thornton, who was mentioned in them.[3]

The letters were soon identified as the work of a man named Patrick Joyce. He lived near Barna, where both he and his wife were teachers in the national school. Joyce was in fact the headmaster. On the night of Friday 15 October 1920, a group of armed, masked men made their way to his home at about 11.30 p.m. Heavy footsteps were heard coming up the little avenue outside the house and moments later there was a loud knock on the door and a demand to open up in the name of the military. Joyce and most of the family had already retired for the night, but his son Joseph and his wife were still up. Young Joyce opened the door and was immediately forced into the kitchen at gunpoint, where a sack was placed over his head. The raiders asked where his father was and a few moments later Patrick Joyce was taken from his bedroom. The house was searched for arms and Joyce was ordered to get dressed. As he came out of the bedroom, his daughter, Rita, awoke, and unsure of what was happening clung to her father. The raiders were gentle with her and told her that everything would be all right. They then left the house with Joyce and told his wife and son not to leave until morning.

At first light Joseph Joyce cycled quickly to the nearest RIC barracks and reported what had happened. Lorry loads of Auxiliaries and Tans immediately made their way to Barna and began searching the area, but no trace of Joyce or his abductors could be found. The search continued over the following days with no success. On Saturday the military again arrived in force, this time employing an armoured car in the search. That afternoon they stopped a man named Thomas MacDonagh from Cappagh while he was cycling home. The Tans questioned him regarding the whereabouts of Joyce and when he replied that he did not know, he was beaten and had his bicycle smashed. They also shot a cow belonging to a local farmer. Another man, Tom Carr, also from Cappagh, was stopped and questioned, and because he was unable to help the Tans with their enquiries, he was shot in the leg and left lying on the road. Luckily, some neighbours took him to hospital, where his wound was treated. The Tans questioned Dominic Fegan from the same area and he was kicked and beaten for not telling them what they wanted to hear. Before leaving, they warned Fegan that if Joyce was not released by 8 p.m. the following evening, they would come back and shoot him. Fegan replied bravely that they might as well shoot him there and then as he had no idea of Joyce's whereabouts and knew nothing about the men who had kidnapped him. A police constable then interrupted the Tans and was instrumental in having Fegan released. Fegan walked into Galway to have his wounds treated at the hospital. As he made his way home later, he was again attacked by the Tans, but the constable again came to his aid and he got home safely. The Saturday market in Galway was also disrupted by the military and people fled in terror; however, the only casualty was a dog, which was shot dead.

At 12.30 p.m. on Monday 18 October, the Auxiliaries and

Tans entered the Moycullen Co-operative Store and ordered the manager, Laurence Tallon, and the shop assistants, both men and women, outside at gunpoint. They lined them up against the wall of the store and questioned them about Joyce. When they did not get the information requested, the Tans ordered two of the assistants, Tim O'Connor and Walter MacDonagh, to remove their clothing. They were both flogged for about five minutes with a leather strap. The military then turned their attention to Laurence Tallon and warned him that if Joyce was not released by midnight they would shoot 100 Sinn Féiners. Tallon and the others were then ordered to go back to work. As Tallon was going back into the store, one of the Tans shot him in the back of the head, and then began shooting through the windows of the building. Luckily, no one else was hit. On their way back into Galway, the Auxiliaries and Tans stopped at a bog where three men, William Connolly, John Cullinan and Pat Walsh, were working. These men were also ordered to strip and were beaten severely, and Connolly was shot. Connolly and Tallon were taken to hospital in Galway and both survived.[4]

If the IRA was in any doubt about Patrick Joyce, the reaction of the Tans and Auxiliaries certainly proved his value to them, which at the same time indicated his guilt. This, and other evidence that the republicans had built up, meant that action could be taken. The letters Togher passed on to his colleagues were also damning for Joyce, as they implicated a number of local people, including Michael Thornton and Fr Michael Griffin, in republican activities by naming them. The following is an extract from one letter: 'these men who joined the Volunteers did so because they were being encouraged by Curates Griffin and O'Meehan who kept telling them that men should never be afraid or scared, that it was only women and children who suffered fear'. In another letter, to Sir Hamar Greenwood, Joyce wrote, 'You do not know me personally but I was well known to your predecessor in that office, Sir Ian MacPherson. Up to now I have not disguised my handwriting, but from now on I will sign myself "45" in any letter to the Chief Secretary.' In a letter to the OC of the Tans he requested him to send his men to Barna and to 'confiscate the Colgan house', the home of Delia Colgan, principal of the girls' school in Barna, whose husband, Matthew, had resigned from the RIC and become a supporter of the IRA. A number of other local men were also named in Joyce's letters.

A meeting of the Connemara Brigade Staff was held, during which the letters were read out. The men around the table found it difficult to believe someone they felt was honourable would betray them. It was decided to think about the situation before coming to a decision. Another meeting was arranged at which it was decided to contact General Mulcahy, Chief of Staff of the Provisional Government in Dublin, who gave them permission to court-martial Patrick Joyce. His fate was sealed.

The courthouse was an unroofed cabin near Lissagardawn, Connemara, and four judges sat for the trial. The evidence was presented and Joyce admitted that the letters had been written by him. After some deliberation the following verdict was read:

'By decree of the Provisional Government of Ireland, Patrick Joyce, having been found guilty of spying for the crown forces was sentenced to death by shooting.' When Joyce was told the verdict, he appealed to the court and asked to be released to his family, giving his word of honour that he would never do any harm again. The judges listened to the appeal, but had a major concern: Joyce now knew each of them, which could prove detrimental to their own safety if he was released.

The sentence was to be carried out and Fr Tommy Burke, the curate from Glencorrib, was summoned. He remained with Joyce until his execution. Joyce was buried in an unmarked grave in a nearby bog. His five letters were placed in a bottle and then buried in another location in the bog.

By the end of the week, all hope of finding Patrick Joyce alive had faded, and his wife was pleading for his body to be handed over to the family. The IRA leaked a message to the family to assure them that his spiritual needs had been looked after and that a priest had administered the last rites to him. The Tans, however, believed that Fr Griffin had been the priest who had attended Joyce, which proved fatal for him. In fact, Fr Griffin had been unaware of what had actually happened, and had gone to visit Mrs Joyce to try to comfort her over her missing husband. He had also publicly prayed for the safe return of Patrick Joyce during Sunday mass and had visited the Furbo and Barna schools and spoken with the teachers and the children. Before leaving Furbo, he had been warned by one of the assistant teachers to be careful, as he had access to information that Fr Griffin was a marked man. This obviously disturbed him, as he mentioned it to the principal of the girls' school in Barna.[5]

Joe Togher's work for the IRA was vital and the authorities were now extremely worried about how the republicans were getting information. Togher was also working an intelligence service outside the post office, via two of the favourite haunts of the Tans and Auxiliaries: the Skeffington Arms in Eyre Square and Baker's Hotel in Eyre Street. He was ordered to frequent these places, which he found 'distasteful', but it was his duty to make contacts and relay any information back to his OC. His visits proved fruitful and he made three contacts, two military and one civilian, over several weeks, and gained information on troop movements. He also made contact with two other useful agents, a Miss Carter in the County Club and George Cunniffe in the Railway Hotel.

The British had set up a centralised intelligence department in Dominick Street, with a Captain Keating as the OC. This department had authority over all the other military establishments, including the army, RIC, Tans and Auxiliaries. All information was to be pooled together in this department so that nothing was missed when investigating the republicans. Keating was heard to boast in the County Club that he would 'walk the Shinners into it'. However, Togher had a friend, Michael Brennan, an ex-British Army officer, who was also friendly with Keating. This proved extremely useful to Togher, as he was now getting vital information about British agents who were travelling the roads dressed as tramps, trying to pick up on local gossip. They could be used to provide

Keating with misinformation. Togher also had a contact in the National Bank named Kirwan, who supplied him with information about Keating's bank details. He was almost always overdrawn on his account and the IRA felt this might be useful – perhaps they could buy information from him. This move was not successful, but it was worth the effort, as it proved to Keating what he was up against.

Through his intelligence contacts, Togher was able to compile a list of home addresses in England of British Army and Auxiliaries serving in Galway.[6] The IRA were attempting to gather as much information about these men as possible, should they ever need to track them down.

A number of young men who were working at the Railway Hotel came under suspicion and were arrested, among them Patrick Spelman from Suckeen who was gathering information for Togher. He later married Mary Burke from Athenry, who also worked at the hotel, and she remembered watching from a hotel window as the men were marched away with their hands held above their heads.[7]

17

The Murder of Fr Griffin

On the morning of Sunday 14 November 1920, Fr Michael Griffin cycled from his house in Montpellier Terrace to say mass, first in Furbo and then in Barna. Fr Griffin was born on 18 September 1892 in Gurteen, near Ballinasloe. He was ordained a priest in April 1917 and just over a year later he became a curate in Rahoon. He was a nationalist and his sympathies lay with the Sinn Féin movement, but he believed that an independent Ireland should be gained only by peaceful means. In contrast, his friend and colleague Fr John O'Meehan was deeply involved with the nationalist movement and was known for his connection to it. He also lived at Montpellier Terrace. When the Black and Tans arrived in Galway they warned Fr O'Meehan that he was a marked man and very high on their list. Because of this, he had to go into hiding each night in a private hospital in the same terrace. This resulted in Fr Griffin being on duty for sick calls at night. Their parish duty covered St Joseph's, Rahoon and St Mary's College, as far as Barna and Furbo.

Fr Griffin left early on that Sunday morning as the first

mass was at 9 a.m. It was a cold, windy November day with showers making the journey uncomfortable. Fr Griffin prayed and asked for the safe return of Patrick Joyce at both masses. It was almost midday when he returned home and had something to eat. At 4.30 in the afternoon he walked to St Joseph's church and on the way had a game of football with some youngsters. After he returned home, Fr O'Meehan left for his safe house. That evening some other priests arrived as usual for a game of cards with Fr Griffin. The card games finished at about 10.30 p.m. and the priests left the house, waved off by Fr Griffin. He retired to bed at 11 p.m.

At about midnight, some men arrived at his house. He did not hear the first knocks on the front door, but they got louder, disturbing the people next door. A short time later, Fr Griffin awoke and went to the window to investigate the noise. His housekeeper, Barbara King, also awoke and heard Fr Griffin calling out the window, asking who was there. She then heard him say, 'All right, I'll be down in a minute.' Some moments later, she heard him say, 'I would do the same for anyone.' It was later proven that she could not have heard this conversation had he been talking outside the house, so it was believed that Fr Griffin had admitted whoever called to the house that night.

Willie Mulvagh, the man who lived next door, had looked out the window when the knocking began and had seen three men at the door. He had thought he heard Fr Griffin say, 'Come on up.' About ten minutes later, the men all left together, and Fr Griffin pulled the door closed behind him.

They walked off into a wet and windy night. Thus began the biggest mystery of the Galway War of Independence.[1]

It seems that Fr Griffin had been lured from the house by British forces or someone aiding them. He was taken to Lenaboy Castle, where he was questioned. After being interrogated, he was shot through the head and died instantly. The question remains as to whether this was an accident or murder. There has been much speculation as to who actually killed Fr Griffin.

Earlier that night a raid had taken place at the home of the Kennedy family in Salthill. Three armed men dressed in civilian clothes had entered the house, demanding to know the whereabouts of the 'Professor'. This was the pseudonym of Thomas Ó Maille, who was known to the authorities as a subversive. They were trying to arrest him, but Ó Maille was not there at the time. The family was terrified, and there were children sleeping upstairs. The men waved their guns about and referred to each other by the names Barker, Smith and Ward. They also mentioned that they had a 'terrible job' to do later on that night. After a time, the three men left the house and made their way back in the direction of the town.

Geraldine Plunkett Dillon, sister of 1916 leader Joseph Plunkett, later stated in her memoir that she watched events unfolding at the Kennedys' home from a house nearby. She also remembered that later a lorry drove by both houses at speed:

> It was a terrible night, the wind was lifting puddles off the road in sheets and splashing it down again a few yards on ... Some

time afterwards, about an hour, a lorry came by at a terrible belt. I stepped back behind the curtains, as a face at a window might get a bullet. A short time later an outside car went by with the three men in it. The lorry had the body of Fr Griffin and the three men, Barker, Smith and Ward, were his murderers. The cook in Lenaboy Castle told me later that the Tans in the lorry had refused to go any further with the body unless these three men went with them. I did not know about Fr Griffin at the time, but it was plain that something hideous was going on.

Dillon also claimed that it was a Galway RIC Constable who lured Fr Griffin out of the house that night.[2]

The following morning there was an anniversary mass for a former bishop of Galway, which all the local clergy were supposed to attend. One of the priests, Fr O'Dea, noticed that Fr Griffin was not present and when mass finished he cycled to Montpellier Terrace to find out if anything was wrong. Barbara King explained that Fr Griffin had been called out the previous night and had not returned. Fr O'Dea made a quick inspection of the house and immediately noticed that the Holy Oils and Blessed Sacrament were still in the tabernacle. This meant that Fr Griffin could not have gone out on a sick call – he would have taken these items with him. Fr O'Dea then sent a telegram to every priest within a twenty-mile radius of the city asking if anyone knew the whereabouts of Fr Griffin. By mid-afternoon it was clear that no one knew where he was. Dr Thomas O'Dea, the Bishop of Galway, was informed that Fr Griffin was missing. Many were convinced that he had been kidnapped and suspected the crown forces.

District Inspector Richard Cruise was contacted and he said that he would have his men carry out a search for Fr Griffin. He also said that he would not accept that crown forces would abduct a priest.

News of Fr Griffin's abduction hit the streets of the city on the morning of 16 November. People were stunned. Police patrols began searching all surrounding areas. A waitress working in Teach na Mbia (later Taaffe's Shop) reported to the priest in College House in Lombard Street (parish priests' housing) that she had overheard one Tan saying to another that 'There was a bloody parson shot last night.' Another girl, Chrissie Lyons, was visiting a friend, Della Hession, whose parents had a pub in Mary Street. The Tans used to frequent the pub and they were there that night. Chrissie overheard one of them say, 'The parson is in the bog.' Chrissie was the daughter of Head Constable Daniel Lyons, the man who had warned Michael Walsh that he was a marked man. She told her father what she had heard in the pub, and Lyons then leaked the information to the clergy. The issue was also raised in the House of Commons, where it was also denied that crown forces had any role in the disappearance of the missing priest.

Rumours and speculation were rife throughout the town that week. Then on Saturday afternoon, at about 3 p.m., William Duffy of Cloughscoiltia, a mile and a half north of Barna village, noticed the outline of a grave as he drove cattle into a field. He went for help and returned with some friends. They began digging until they uncovered a body lying face-down in the bog. Upon turning the remains over, they immediately recognised Fr Griffin. One of the men went to Montpellier Terrace and informed Fr O'Meehan, who was overcome with grief. A short time later he went and informed Canon Davis and other members of the clergy. The remains of Fr Griffin were then taken to St Joseph's church. A post mortem was performed on 21 November, which revealed that Fr Griffin had been shot through the head from the right side. The bullet had passed through his brain and an exit wound was found on the left temple.[3] Brigadier General Chaplain, commanding the Western Division, called on the bishop and expressed his horror and indignation on behalf of the military at the murder of Fr Griffin. He said that he hoped the priests and people would co-operate with the authorities in every way to bring the guilty persons to justice. The county inspector of the RIC also called and expressed his and his men's horror.[4]

Although people were accustomed to hearing of shootings, the murder of a priest shocked the entire town. Again, there was much speculation regarding the killing, but it was believed to have been in reprisal for the kidnapping and execution of Patrick Joyce. Fr Griffin's death was announced at all masses on Sunday 21 November. In St Joseph's church, Canon Davis made his way to the altar and said, 'There is great sorrow in this parish today, sorrow in which you and I will equally share. The body of Fr Griffin with a bullet through his head was found last night.' A shudder of horror swept through the congregation and was followed by agonising moans. That afternoon, Bishop O'Dea condemned the murder, but also

The funeral of Seán Mulvoy and Seamus Quirke.
(Courtesy of Tom Kenny)

Handover of Renmore Barracks, Galway, to the army of the Republic
of Ireland by British forces, February 1922. The men are from the 4th
Battalion, 2nd Brigade, First Western Division. *From left to right:* Henry
Lynch, John Brannigan, John Canavan, Patrick White, Michael Francis,
Joseph Kelly, Patrick Feeney and Sergeant Thomas Kelly (in charge of
the Guard). *(Courtesy of Tom Kenny)*

Eileen Quinn from Kiltartan.
(Courtesy of John Quinn)

Liam Mellows, commander of the
1916 rebellion in Galway.
*(Courtesy of Johnny and Sheila
Molloy)*

Commandant Seán Broderick
(Galway city).
(Courtesy of Helen Spelman)

Malachy Quinn with his three
children, Alfie, Tessie and Eva.
(Courtesy of John Quinn)

Above: Commandant Louis D'Arcy (Headford).
(Courtesy of Daniel Callaghan)

Left: Tom Courtney.
(Courtesy of the Courtney family)

Castlegar Flying Column 1920.
Front from left: Thomas 'Baby' Duggan, Christy Courtney, Brian Malloy, Martin Gannon.
Second row, from left: Padraic Feeney, John Tynan, Patrick Glynn, Michael Cunningham. *(Courtesy of Tom Joe Furey)*

James Traynor.
(Author's collection)

Thomas and Margaret Egan.
(Courtesy of Alfie McNamara)

John O'Hanlon.
(Courtesy of William O'Hanlon)

Commandant Thomas
'Baby' Duggan.
(Courtesy of Tom Joe Furey)

Commandant Thomas Powell.
(Courtesy of Seathran Powell)

Michael Walsh.
(Courtesy of Padraic Walsh)

The funeral of Thomas 'Sweeney' Newell.
(Courtesy of Tom Joe Furey)

Pat Margetts and his wife Kathy.
(Courtesy of Jonathan Margetts)

Captain Brian Molloy wearing his prison hat. *(Courtesy of Johnny and Sheila Molloy)*

The RIC barracks in Eglington Street, Galway.
(Courtesy of Tommy Holohan)

Old IRA attending the parade for the unveiling of the Castlegar Monument. *(Courtesy of Tom Joe Furey)*

Éamon de Valera inspecting a parade of the Old IRA in Galway. *From right:* Mr Birmingham, Matt Hackett, John Melia, and the seventh man is Martin Lally. *(Courtesy of Barbara Shally)*

Fr Michael Griffin.
*(Courtesy of the late
Fr Robert E. Lee)*

Margaret 'Peg' Broderick.
(Courtesy of Tom Kenny)

The body of one of the Loughnane brothers
before burial.
(Courtesy of Daniel Callaghan)

called for restraint. He also sent his secretary to Gurteen to inform Fr Griffin's family that his body had been found.

The funeral took place on 22 November and from early morning crowds gathered in St Joseph's church. Over 12,000 people could not gain entry and knelt on the road and pavement outside; many more attended mass in other churches around the city. The funeral mass began at 11.30 a.m. and was celebrated by two bishops, an archbishop and 150 priests. Following the mass the funeral moved off through the streets of the city. The route crossed O'Brien's bridge where the RIC lined up, removed their caps, stood to attention and saluted the cortège as it passed. The procession then made its way through Shop Street, around by Eyre Square and up Forster Street towards Moneenageesha, where a motor vehicle was waiting to take the remains to Loughrea for burial. The streets were practically free of military, and thousands of mourners followed in procession.[5] While few or no Tans or Auxiliaries were present, a group was in Forster Street as the funeral passed. A young woman, Katie Larkin, shouted abuse and waved a tricolour at them, saying that they would 'rot in hell' for what they had done. One of the men shouted back at her, 'Shut up you bitch, it was your own that did it.' This certainly gave credence to another rumour that Fr Griffin was lured from his residence by someone speaking Irish.[6]

The military inquiry that followed concluded with the following verdict: 'The late Rev. Michael Griffin, C.C., Galway died on or about November 15th 1920 at or near Clough-scoiltia, near Barna, Co. Galway, as a result of a gunshot in the head, fired furiously, willfully and with malice aforethought by some person or persons unknown and that such person or persons unknown were guilty of murder.' The court then expressed its sincere sympathy to the relatives and many friends of the deceased.[7]

The reasons behind the abduction and murder have remained somewhat of a mystery to present times and there is still speculation as to who was responsible. However, most sources indicate that Fr Griffin was murdered in reprisal for the killing of Patrick Joyce. It has been suggested that Fr O'Meehan was the intended target that night, but he had already left the house when the killers arrived.[8] According to Joe Togher's witness statement, the two people involved in the abduction of Fr Griffin were a man named Nichols and William Joyce, later known as Lord Haw Haw and hanged by the British following the Second World War for treason. Joyce was known to have acted as a scout for the Tans and Auxiliaries. In a statement, Togher said that it was Joyce who had actually called Fr Griffin out that night on the pretence of a sick call. Togher later intercepted a letter from Joyce to an Auxiliary officer, but this was uncovered after the Truce was signed in 1921. Togher later stated that had they uncovered the information earlier, they would have shot Joyce.[9]

Shortly after the Truce was signed Tom Kenny, editor of the *Connacht Tribune*, interviewed Inspector Cruise in Eglinton Street Barracks. During the discussion, Cruise said that Fr Griffin was shot in Lenaboy Castle, but that it had been an accident: the gun had gone off while he was being interrogated. However, the shooting must have taken place in the grounds, as the spent bullet, having passed through Fr Griffin's head, shattered a window in the Dominican Convent nearby and was found on the window sill by Sr Bernard Heuston, a sister of the executed 1916 patriot Seán Heuston.[10]

Pat Margetts later recorded that a warning 'Doomed R.I.P. Amen' was posted on the house where Fr Griffin lived. Margetts had gone to pay his respects and looked out of place as he filed past the coffin in military uniform. He always maintained that the authorities knew who was responsible, but nothing was done to bring anyone to justice.[11]

In 1931 a man named Michael Francis Kelly-Mor from Loughrea was working in the Valuation Office in Ely Place in Dublin. He later gave a witness statement regarding a conversation he had while working there. He mentioned that his work colleagues included three men surnamed Reilly, Carthy and Morris. One day during the course of conversation he spoke about the terrible murder of Fr Griffin in Galway. This prompted an immediate reaction from Morris, who said: 'That Bastard got what he deserved, and there was another man there too we were looking for, and he'd have got the same if we found him.' He then left the room. It was generally known that Morris had been a member of the Black and Tans or the Auxiliaries, and he had never denied his involvement in the force. Kelly-Mor was shocked by what Morris had said and asked the other two men to go to the authorities with him and make a statement on the matter. Both refused. A few days later he met Morris near St Stephen's Green and offered him £10 for information regarding the exact details on the abduction and murder of Fr Griffin. Morris was tempted, saying that he would think about the offer, but then refused. The matter was never again raised between the two men.[12]

In more recent times, in the early 1970s, a young man walking in the grounds of Lenaboy Castle met an old English man. They spoke to each other and during the conversation the old man mentioned that he had served in the Auxiliaries during the troubles. He also said that he remembered Fr Griffin and that the shooting had been an accident.[13] Still another source states that when General Crozier was appointed to command the Auxiliaries he was disgusted by the lawlessness of the force and the crimes being committed: 'A Galway priest who had been invited to America to give evidence of an attempt by the Auxies to make a raping assault upon a nunnery … was murdered by the Auxies and his body was thrown into a bog.'[14]

In November 1922 a monument was erected at Clough-scoiltia on the spot where Fr Griffin's body was found and a wreath-laying ceremony takes place there annually. In 1937 a road was named in Fr Griffin's memory.

18

Murder of the Loughnane Brothers

On Friday 26 November 1920, Patrick and Harry Loughnane were arrested by the Black and Tans while threshing corn on the family farm in Shanaglish, Beagh. The Tans first questioned the men in the field, asking them if they were nationalists. The brothers admitted to being members of Sinn Féin. The Tans then forced the Loughnane brothers into the back of an army lorry.[1] James Carroll, a cousin of the brothers, was helping them at the time and was also arrested, but was later separated from his cousins. He eventually ended up in Rath Camp in the Curragh.[2]

Patrick Loughnane was secretary of the local Sinn Féin branch; he was also active in the local GAA. His younger brother, Harry, was president of the local Sinn Féin club and goalkeeper with Beagh hurling club. Both young men were held in the highest regard in the south Galway area.[3] Harry Loughnane was twenty-two and had been studying to be a teacher in the de La Salle College in Waterford, but had to abandon his studies for health reasons. Patrick, who was two years older, was a welder by trade.[4]

The brothers were taken to Gort Bridewell, where they were tortured and beaten for several hours. They were then bound together, tied to the tailgate of a military lorry and dragged along the country roads to Drumharsna Castle, headquarters of the Auxiliary forces and the Tans in that area. They were subjected to further assaults and at 11 p.m. were taken from the castle to Moyvilla Woods. At a location just off the public road, both men were shot.[5]

On Saturday morning Mrs Loughnane, a widow, accompanied by a local priest, Fr Nagle, went to Gort Barracks to enquire about her sons. She was told that the Auxiliaries had taken them away on the previous night and that they had no more information on their whereabouts.[6] On Sunday morning, Auxiliaries arrived at the wood and removed the bodies. A short time later they dumped the bodies at another location, Umbriste, about three miles from Ardrahan, and set fire to them. Apparently not satisfied with the results, they tried to bury the remains, but on account of the rocky soil they failed. As a last resort they threw the bodies into a muddy pond close by, where they hoped they would not be discovered. To make detection more difficult, they poured burned and dirty oil into the water.[7]

At midday on Monday the Auxiliaries raided the Loughnane home and told the boys' mother that her sons had escaped and that they were conducting a search for them. Mrs Loughnane was alone, except for her niece. Her husband was dead and her daughters Norah, a teacher in Currandulla

National School, and Katie, a teacher in Corofin, were both living away from home. She had another son, but he was living in England. The day after the raid, Norah travelled to Galway and made enquiries at the police barracks in Eglinton Street, but was told that her brothers were not in custody there. She then made enquiries at Galway in the hope that they were being held in prison, but again the authorities had no information. Norah then made her way to one of the most dreaded places in Galway at the time, Lenaboy Castle, to talk with the Auxiliaries. She was brought into the castle, where the commanding officer met with her. He told her that her brothers had indeed been arrested, but that they had escaped along with eight other rebels and they were 'wanted men'. One of the rebels had been recaptured, but the others, including her brothers, were 'running south'. He was very courteous towards her and took her name and address, informing her that if he had any additional information he would contact her directly.

Both family and friends became increasingly anxious about the fate of the brothers. They knew that if the boys had indeed escaped, they would have managed to get word to them somehow.

It was ten days after their initial arrest that the bodies of the brothers were discovered. A young man, Michael Loughnane, a relative of the brothers, dreamed that the bodies would be found in water. The dream returned every night until he made his way to the correct location and there discovered the bodies lying in about a three-feet depth of water, submerged and hidden from view.[8] When, at the later inquest, he was asked about his knowing the exact location of the bodies, he replied, 'Harry came to me in my sleep and he asked me to go to a certain place, which he pointed out.'[9] The remains of the brothers were taken to a barn near Kinvara and the family was informed. Norah went to identify the bodies, and although they were largely unrecognisable, she managed to identify Harry. She later stated that Patrick's face had been blown off and that she could only recognise him by his shoulders, as he was broader than Harry.[10] A local doctor examined the remains carefully and, although they were badly burned, he was able to identify the letters 'I V', which had been cut into the charred flesh in several places. Two of Harry's fingers were missing and his right arm was broken at the shoulder and almost severed completely from the body. The brothers' skulls were fractured in a number of places and part of Patrick's skull was missing. The doctor stated that both Patrick's wrists and legs were broken and noted that explosives may have been placed in the men's mouths.[11] Fr Nagle said, 'I have been through the African war. I have been everywhere that a soul required my services and a worse thing than this I never saw.'

The remains of the brothers were brought to Shanaglish Church where the funeral mass took place. Before the bodies were taken away for burial, a party of police, Auxiliaries and military arrived at the church and had the coffins opened to view the remains. This was a harrowing sight, particularly for the family. All the military authorities continued to deny any involvement in the murders, even at the inquiry held later. Following the mass, eight men shouldered each coffin and, followed by huge crowds, made their way to the local cemetery where the Loughnane brothers were laid to rest side by side. As soon as the last sods had been placed in position, six local IRA volunteers stepped forward and fired three volleys over the graves. This final tribute to the men was also a symbol of defiance and a message to crown forces that their bloodiest efforts only strengthened resistance against them.[12]

The following poem appeared in the newspapers, alongside the report on the Loughnane brothers. It was written by a girl named Agnes O'Farrelly.

The Truce of God

The Truce of God we ask; a time,
When men may look – If they dare,
Into the cavern grim and bare,
Where each man reckons with his soul.

Give us God's Truce! a breathing space,
To count the still unnumbered dead,
And fix our gaze, now blurred and red,
On all the morrows yet unborn.

A truce to kill the rusting doubt,
That sears our will; to lift the ban,
That we may speak as man to man,
And know that God and truth abide.

A pause to still our panting hearts,
And staunch the life-blood's ceaseless drain,
To figure out the cost; the pain,
The widow's wail; the mother's tears.

> The very earth is clogged with blood,
> And horror-seated men are numb;
> From veins grow cold; and limb and dumb,
> For none may speak as freemen speak.
>
> Speak! England! Speak! for yours the sin,
> And yours the force to work your way;
> Your dead and ours cry out today,
> An outraged God awaits your voice![13]

That some British Army officers were appalled at the indiscipline of the Tans, and the effect on their own soldiers when they were in contact with them, is borne out by an earlier incident in late September involving Pat Margetts. One night Margetts set up a machine-gun post at Eyre Square with orders to stop anyone suspicious or breaking curfew. The soldiers manning the position were invited to Eglinton Street Barracks by the Tans for a drink. Margetts decided to let a number of the soldiers take up the Tans' offer, but ordered them not to stay past a certain length of time. After about an hour, Margetts felt that his men should have returned to the machine-gun post. He proceeded to Eglinton Street Barracks alone and ordered them to return. He experienced some difficulty, as they were very reluctant to go back, but they had no choice – this was a direct order. One RIC sergeant followed them outside and began to verbally abuse Margetts. At first Margetts ignored him, but after the sergeant insulted Margetts' Scottish heritage, a fist fight broke out, during which Margetts gave a good account of himself. He then returned with his men to Eyre Square. Furious, he gave the offending soldiers a good dressing down.

As his temper subsided, he heard the sound of a Crossley Tender coming from the direction of Eglinton Street. It turned into Williamsgate Street and proceeded towards Eyre Square. Margetts called out 'Halt!' in a loud voice, but the driver failed to acknowledge the order. Margetts again ordered the vehicle to halt, but again the driver continued to move forward. Suddenly the sound of machine-gun fire was heard throughout the streets as the soldier manning the weapon opened fire. The Crossley halted immediately, within a few feet of Margetts. The inspector from Eglinton Street Barracks emerged, furious, but Margetts calmly told him that he had disobeyed a direct order from an officer of the crown, forcing his men to take immediate action. The inspector calmed down and was forced to apologise before being allowed to proceed on his journey. However, the following day, Margetts was reprimanded and pulled off curfew duty.[14] As far as can be ascertained, this was the only time during the War of Independence that crown forces turned guns on each other intentionally.

Margetts was bitterly disappointed by the murder now taking place across the city and county and like other level-headed people hoped for an end to the bloodshed. However, by December 1920 there was little sign of a truce; in fact there was increasing activity by the authorities in Galway, with the Town Hall being commandeered by the British in an attempt to house prisoners there. An internment camp was set up in the area in front of the building where suspects were held until decisions were made regarding their sentencing. The camp was also receiving IRA prisoners from County Mayo.[15] Raids on houses continued and the Galway Workhouse was targeted.[16] A number of men were taken into custody: Martin Crowe of Bohermore, Frank Henry of Market Street, Patrick O'Connor of Abbeygate Street, Peter Flaherty of Barna, James Curran of Spiddal, Michael Ward of Clifden and John Hosty of Shantalla. They were sent to Ballykinlar Internment Camp near Dundrum in County Down.[17]

19

Dublin Shootings and Aran Island Raids

By late 1920 Commandant Joe Howley was OC of the Mid-Galway Brigade. Born in Oranmore in 1895, he was only two years of age when his father died. His mother later married William Keane, the owner of Keane's bar, which was burned during the attack on Oranmore. From this marriage, Joe gained two stepsisters, Josie and Madge, and a stepbrother, Willie. Joe was educated in the local national school and later in St Joseph's Secondary School in Galway. Even as a teenager, he was a dedicated nationalist, and joined the Irish Volunteers at eighteen years of age. He was a popular young man and his commitment saw him progress through the ranks. He helped prepare the men for the 1916 rebellion.

Following the events of 1916, Howley was sentenced to five years' penal servitude in Dartmoor Prison. He was released towards the end of 1917 and immediately set about organising the local Volunteers. Some of the meetings took place in the bar. After the attack on Oranmore in August 1920 during which his home (Keane's bar) was burned, Howley was forced to go on the run or face almost certain death. Local people said that he was a 'marked man' since the ambush at Merlin Park. While Howley was on the run he stayed at a number of safe locations, one being the curate's house in Clarinbridge, where Fr Kenny, who later became parish priest in Oranmore, was resident.

One night Howley and another republican, Paddy Mullins, were in the kitchen with Fr Kenny when there was a knock on the door. Fr Kenny said that he wasn't expecting any visitors and that it could either be someone in trouble or the British. Howley and Mullins checked their guns while the priest answered the door. Standing there were a number of British soldiers who requested permission to search the house. Fr Kenny invited them into the parlour and asked them to do as they wished 'silently' as his housekeeper was asleep upstairs. He began talking to them about the Great War and how he had wanted to join the forces fighting in France. During the conversation, the soldiers relaxed, and after a few minutes apologised for disturbing him and left.

On 5 December 1920, Howley and Mullins travelled to Dublin by train to enquire about a consignment of arms that had gone missing. Upon arrival at Broadstone Station in the capital, the men separated. According to one source, as Howley walked along the platform, his name was called out by members of the 'Dublin Castle Murder Gang', as the Cairo Gang, a group of British intelligence agents who had been sent to Dublin during the Irish War of Independence in order to conduct operations against the IRA, was known to some. As he turned, they opened fire, hitting him a number of times and killing him instantly.[1]

However, there are other versions of the story of how Joe Howley was killed. The second states that he left the station with a Dublin contact. It was about 5.30 in the evening and it was dark. As the two men crossed the bridge, making their way towards the city centre, a number of shots rang out and Howley fell, mortally wounded. His companion ran and disappeared into the darkness. An eyewitness reported that he heard four gunshots and saw a tall man dressed in civilian clothing fall on the left side of the bridge. Immediately afterwards he heard a whistle being sounded and a motor car approached at speed. A number of men jumped into the car and it drove away quickly towards the city. Some of the passengers who had emerged from the station rushed to the injured man's aid. One of them was a lady who tried in vain to stem the flow of blood with a scarf, while a number of people began reciting prayers for the dying man. The fire brigade ambulance was contacted and arrived soon afterwards. Howley was lifted onto a stretcher and placed in the ambulance. As it was about to be driven away, an armoured car arrived on the scene and a number of soldiers surrounded the ambulance, preventing it from moving. The officer commanding then spoke with the ambulance driver and after a few minutes Howley was transferred to the armoured car. He was supposed to be taken to King George V Hospital, but instead he was taken to Dublin Castle. When enquiries were made at the hospital regarding Howley, the medical authorities stated that he had not been admitted. Dublin Castle simply stated that they had 'no communication whatever to make' regarding Howley. However, he was eventually taken to the hospital, dying of the gunshot wounds to his head and body, and was accompanied by a priest, Fr Headley, OP.

A third story concerning his death was later reported by Dublin Castle:

> A patrol was waiting for 'wanted' men at Broadstone Station on Saturday evening. Their orders were to arrest any 'wanted' person at or leaving the station. One of the constables recognised a man named Howley, who was known to be a desperate Sinn Féiner and who has long been 'on the run.' The constables followed until he separated from the rest of the passengers leaving the station. One constable stepped forward to carry out the arrest, while a second man covered him from possible attack. There is usually a picquet of Sinn Féiners at the station and well known criminals often have armed escorts. Howley was accompanied by another man. When the constable carrying out the arrest seized Howley he broke away and dived on one side, at the same time putting his hand in his pocket. The man who was with him took to his heels. Both the constable carrying out the arrest and the constable covering him fired at Howley, and one of them fired twice after the second man. On these patrols it is arranged that a car is always handy in order to take persons who are arrested into custody. The car drove up at a pre-arranged signal. The constables entered it and came straight to headquarters. Military with an armoured car were sent out and soon brought in the body. A military inquiry in lieu of an inquest was held on Monday.

On Monday morning Howley's remains were taken to Berkley Road church and his coffin was draped in the tricolour and similar-coloured ribbons were tied to the wreaths. A special mass was celebrated in the church on Tuesday morning and masses were said across all the churches in Dublin that morning for the repose of his soul. At 12 p.m. his remains were removed from the church and taken to Broadstone Station for the train journey home to Oranmore. When the train pulled into Oranmore Station that evening it was met by a large force of military and police. The officer commanding removed the flag from the coffin and also had the tricolour ribbons removed from the wreaths. The remains were then handed over to Howley's family and friends and taken to the village church, followed closely by the military and the police. His funeral mass took place the following morning. His uncles, Joseph Heneghan and Peter and John Rabbitt, stood with the coffin, as did his cousins, Charlie Rabbitt and Patrick and Martin Hanley. His mother was supported by her sisters, Mrs Rabbitt and Mrs Devaney. Following the mass, there was also a military presence as the funeral cortège moved towards the cemetery for burial.[2]

There was a definite sense of outrage among the people, particularly after the 'official' account of the killing was released by Dublin Castle. There was no doubt that the authorities were aware that Howley would be arriving in Dublin on the evening train and they were going to target and kill him. The question was, how did they know? When Michael Collins received news of Howley being killed, he was furious. He issued orders to all units in Dublin to locate the man responsible, saying, 'We'll make a Brigadier General out of the man who captures him.'[3]

A somewhat strange story was told following Joe Howley's death. It seems that a few days after he was killed, a number of his IRA colleagues who were also on the run witnessed what they later believed to be a warning from beyond the grave. They were at their hideout in Bushfield near Oranmore. On this bright, moonlit night, two of the men emerged from the underground shelter to go on sentry duty. Both men said that they saw Joe Howley standing close to a wall beside them, dressed in full Irish Volunteer uniform. They were stunned and returned to inform the others. The men were unnerved and decided to move to a new location immediately – a good decision, as the hideout was raided early the following morning.[4]

One of the most notorious Black and Tans in Galway was a man named Eugene Igoe, a native of Mayo. He had served with the RIC initially before transferring to the Tans. He served in Killeen and later in Galway, where he became attracted to Margaret Burke, a member of Cumann na mBan, but she rejected him. Joseph Togher later felt that she should have allowed a friendship to develop, as then they might have been in a position to do 'something about him'. Igoe eventually went to Dublin, where he became part of the infamous Cairo Gang.[5] He was aware of some of the Galway republicans and was suspected of fingering Joseph Howley.

Following the death of Howley, Sweeney Newell was

summoned to Dublin by Michael Collins. He travelled to the capital with Baby Duggan, both on separate IRA business. Upon arrival in Dublin they were met by Stephen Murphy, a friend of Duggan. Another man, Thomas Kilcoyne, also met them and it was he who arranged 'lodgings' for Newell. The following morning Newell was taken to the IRA Intelligence Headquarters, where he met Frank Thornton, one of the officers there. Newell was then detailed to serve with a 'Special Intelligence' unit: he was to identify Igoe, as he had known him in Galway.

Murphy secured a job for Newell in the Dublin whiskey distillery. In the evenings, two men, Dan O'Connell and James Hughes, accompanied Newell during his walks through the main streets, trying to locate Igoe. One evening, while Newell was making his way back to his lodgings alone, he spotted Igoe near Broadstone Station. He immediately returned to headquarters and reported that he had seen him, but there was no trace of him when they returned to the spot. A few days later, he saw him again, this time near Dublin Castle, but again the IRA members were too late in getting to the location. On the third occasion, Newell was again alone, this time in Grafton Street, when he spotted Igoe. He immediately returned to the headquarters in Crow Street. Accompanied by Charles Dalton, Newell began making his way back to Grafton Street. They were followed by the IRA's Dublin active service unit at a safe distance on the opposite side of the street, but it soon fell behind. Dalton and Newell had walked too quickly through Wicklow Street and were well ahead of the unit when they turned onto Grafton Street. They walked directly into a trap and were immediately surrounded by the 'Murder Gang', including Tans. Igoe had also spotted Newell.

There was no time for the men to retreat or to warn their own squad. Igoe grabbed Newell by the collar of his coat and said, 'Come on, Newell, I want you.' Newell and Dalton were taken back to Wicklow Street and made to stand against a wall, where they were questioned for about twenty minutes. The men were then separated and Newell taken to Greek Street, where he was again questioned. The Tans took up positions on the corners of the street, ensuring that there was no means of escape or rescue. Igoe continued the interrogation, asking where Baby Duggan and some others were hiding out. Newell refused to divulge any information. Igoe then told him to run across the street, but he refused, as there were Tans in every direction and he knew they would shoot him. Newell said to Igoe, 'If you want to shoot me, shoot me where I am standing.' Igoe then hit him with a powerful punch, sending him several feet back onto the road. Shooting began immediately and Newell was hit seven times at close range. He collapsed, taking bullets in the hip and legs, and receiving a flesh wound to the stomach. The brutal treatment did not end there. As Newell lay in the road, Igoe sounded a whistle, and within a minute a police van arrived. Newell was thrown onto the back of a lorry and taken to the Bridewell, where he was kicked and beaten. It was incredible that he was still alive, and some hours later he was taken to George V Hospital, where the Tans believed he would die.[6]

After Newell was shot, Joseph Togher got word from GHQ in Dublin asking if it would be possible to have Igoe shot during his visits to Galway, the purpose of which was to see a girl who worked in Giles's pub in the city. However, he only returned once after Newell was shot, and on that occasion was accompanied by armed guards.[7]

***

On 23 December 1920, Éamon de Valera arrived back in Ireland after spending nineteen months in the United States. Although it seems strange that he spent so much time away from his war-torn country, as one source put it, 'no one, least of all Collins, cared either to try to prevent his going or to comment upon the length of his stay there. As ever, de Valera showed a less than noble capacity for making sure he would not be held responsible for hard decisions.'[8] By the time of his arrival, many clergymen were already calling for a truce and were hoping for a ceasefire by Christmas. The Labour Party was also requesting a truce, as was Anglo-Irish unionist Sir Horace Plunkett, who said in Liverpool, 'There cannot be peace while there is frightfulness on both sides … and the Government attitude is bound to fail.'[9] Fr O'Meehan's message to his congregation in St Joseph's Church was, 'The sacrifices of human life already made on both sides have been, one would think, sufficient to induce all men of good-will to seek to propitiate a merciful God by seeking to lay about a reign of righteousness.'[10] The Archbishop of Tuam,

Dr Gilmartin, also called for a Christmas truce. This, he said, was the only way to stop the killings and give time for both sides to come to some agreement. He added that Ireland was grossly misgoverned and told the government that it could create a unique opportunity to reverse its policies regarding Ireland.[11]

However, a truce was not in the pipeline and the military was actually intensifying its efforts against the republicans. At about 10 p.m. on the night of 18 December 1920, some 250 armed police and military carried out a raid on the Aran Islands for republicans on the run.[12] The islands had been evacuated by the RIC in July 1920, but the British suspected that IRA members were using them as a safe haven.[13] The raid was to be a surprise attack and even the forces engaged in the mission were unaware of where they were going until they were on board the cruiser.

The attack force left Galway armed with machine guns and other weaponry, and steamed at full speed to the islands. Upon arrival, some soldiers took up positions in the hills beyond Kilronan on Inis Mor, while their comrades made their way towards the sleepy village in the early hours of the morning. Soon people were awakened from their slumber and a number of suspects were captured. Some who managed to escape made their way towards the hills, where the other British forces were waiting.

It was by now early morning and the first glimmer of daylight saw the republicans moving quickly through the hills. As they got closer to the military, they were fired upon, resulting in the deaths of two men, Laurence MacDonagh and Michael Mannister, and the wounding of a third, Michael Pelly. Eyewitnesses said the shooting was horrendous and they were surprised that many more were not killed. One of them said that he saw a man moving 'rapidly' amongst the rocks, being fired on by a group of soldiers from about 200 yards. The bullets were striking rock all around him as he ran. He believed that the man's name was Folan and that he had escaped from the village. Folan continued his dash for freedom and ran towards a low cliff edge. Without hesitation, he jumped over the cliff, landing in soft boggy ground, and got away, leaving one of his boots and his revolver stuck in the mud.

During the raid a number of weapons were recovered and eleven men were arrested. The prisoners were taken to Galway and interned at the Town Hall camp.[14] Conditions there left a lot to be desired. At least two young prisoners died while in custody there: Patrick Walsh of Hollymount, County Mayo, died from influenza, as did Michael Mullen of Moylough, during the same week in December 1920.[15] The camp was dirty and there was a bad stench. The men were so badly fed that Galway shop assistants donated a shilling a week to purchase food for the prisoners. Some of the prisoners from the Town Hall were transferred to Ballykinlar.[16]

In the course of another raid on the Aran Islands, a young woman, Bridget Dirrane, a member of Cumann na mBan, was arrested. This was another surprise raid, and Bridget had allowed her male colleagues to escape, fearing that they would be shot. She believed that she had a better chance of staying alive and was in the process of burning incriminating documents when the military arrived. One of them grabbed her and forced her against the wall, while the others tried to kick the fire out and retrieve some of the documents, but they were all practically burned at this stage. One of the soldiers then shoved the barrel of his gun into her mouth and said that he would shoot her if she did not give them information on the other republicans. Her courage held and she told them to go ahead and shoot, that if she had a thousand lives, she would give them all for Ireland. They were furious and dragged her from the house. She was first taken to Galway and from there she was to be sent to Dublin for additional interrogation. During her transportation one of the Black and Tans forced her towards the back of the lorry, saying that the boys wanted to have a bit of fun on the way to Galway. Bridget shouted at the officer, saying that if she was not placed in the cab of the truck with the driver and her personal guard, there was a distinct possibility of an ambush. She added that the IRA would not open fire if they saw her in the truck. It did not take the officer long to make up his mind and order his men to place her in the cab.[17]

20

Ambush and Aftermath

In January 1921 Louis D'Arcy, commandant of the Head-ford IRA battalion, contacted Michael Newell to organise a flying column to carry out an attack in his area. Brian Mol-loy gave Newell permission to support D'Arcy and carry out an ambush. Newell chose some fifty men from Castlegar, Claregalway and Cregmore. Eight of the men were armed with Mausers, but only had eight rounds each; the remain-der had shotguns. They marched towards their objective – Kilroe, near Headford – spending that night in an unoc-cupied house. The following morning they made their way to Kilroe and selected their position for an ambush while it was still dark.

It was Tuesday 18 January when Newell placed his main ambush party behind a strong stone wall facing Headford. Behind them lay wild shrubs for some distance. Six men were placed on high ground to act as a covering party. They were ordered not to open fire unless it was to cover the main party if they were forced to retreat. The orders to the main party were simply to fire on the British as they passed.

Shortly after they took up position, an enemy lorry was spotted making its way towards Headford. For some reason, the covering party opened fire before it reached the ambush location. The lorry was knocked out of action and ground to a halt. Newell had not expected the covering party to fire, not only because of his orders, but also because a local man was walking two horses along the road between his men and the enemy. When the firing started, the horses panicked, causing problems for the owner. Because of this, some of the main ambush party held their fire for fear of hitting the civilian, thus the advantage of surprise was lost.

There were about fifteen Auxiliaries in the lorry and they poured out of the vehicle. Some took cover along the roadside, others dived under the lorry for cover. However, two machine gunners remained on the truck and opened fire on the Volunteer positions. The gunfire was intensive. Newell emptied his weapon at the Auxiliaries and threw four bombs, which exploded near the lorry. The Volunteers were already low on ammunition and a few minutes later Newell called a retreat. One of his men was slightly wounded.

The ambush had been planned to be a short, intensive gunfight at close quarters with surprise on the side of the IRA, and they had hoped to inflict as many casualties as possible without wasting their meagre supply of ammunition in long-range shooting. The Auxiliaries suffered six wounded, but got off lightly considering what could have happened if the covering party had followed orders. Newell was annoyed at the outcome of this attack and decided to try to enlist some

Great War veterans in his company, as these men had a lot of military experience.[1]

When the shooting finished, a soldier mounted one of the horses and galloped all the way to Galway to raise the alarm. People looked on in amazement as the mud-spattered soldier galloped through the streets to Eglinton Street Barracks. Reinforcements were sent immediately to the scene of the ambush, but it was too late: the flying column was well out of reach.

The reinforcements then turned their attention to Headford, and it was shortly before midnight when they got there. While an armoured car supported by Crossley Tenders conducted searches and raids in the countryside around Headford, the Auxiliaries began forcing people out of their homes and made them march, with their hands above their heads, up and down the streets. They then proceeded to burn three buildings in Main Street. One belonged to William O'Malley (a publican), one to Richard Geraghty (a postman), and the third was used as a reading room. The Presbytery was also burned down. It was reported that volumes of flames could be seen from villages close to the ambush. The homes of Tobias Joyce, Martin and Peter Dooley, James Craddock, William MacHugh and William Burke were also burned. It was a cold, dry but breezy night and the flames spread quickly. Families were not given time to salvage any of their belongings. Haggards around the countryside were also set alight. Twenty-one-year-old Thomas Collins of Keelkill was shot dead by the military – again, the official army report was 'shot while trying to escape'.[2] The military had taken Collins from his home at gunpoint after asking him his name. His mother followed and saw the Tans hitting her son with their rifles. She tried to stop the attack, but one of the soldiers hit her with his revolver, telling her he would beat her brains out if she did not stay back. They then took Collins away. Mrs Collins heard one of the police say 'Run, run!' and then a number of shots. One of the policemen, speaking with an English accent, said, 'Do not blame me, mother – I did not fire any shot at your son because I am a Catholic.' The following morning Mrs Collins went outside and found her son's body not too far from the house. It was in a shocking state. She was later to attest, 'All his brains and everything were there and I picked them up and put them in my apron. And what more could I do. A lot of his skull bones were broken.'[3]

The Auxiliaries continued to burn homes on the Thursday and Friday. Worse was to follow on the Saturday after the ambush, with another three men being shot dead: Michael Hoade of Caherlistrane; John Kirwan of Ballinastack; and William Walsh of Clydagh, Headford.

Walsh was thirty years old and lived with his brother, two sisters and an aged father. At 9.30 a.m. on Saturday morning two armed men called to the house and ordered the brothers out. There were four lorries outside. The brothers were ordered to walk along the road. Moments later, shots rang out, and William Walsh uttered 'Sweet Jesus' as he fell to the ground, where he died minutes later.

At about 10.30 p.m. the Auxiliaries arrived at the home of

Michael Hoade, where he lived with his sister. He was ordered out of the house. His sister became very frightened and ran to an upstairs window to see what was happening. However, before she got there, she heard seven or eight shots. They had done the same to Michael Hoade – told him to walk away and then shot him. A while later, his lifeless body was carried back to his house by neighbours. Hoade had another sister married to an RIC constable.

Twenty-two-year-old John 'Jim' Kirwan was the next man targeted. Both his parents were over sixty, and he had one brother who was in ill health, so Jim was the main support to his family. At 2.30 p.m. about forty Auxiliaries arrived in the village in lorries. One of the trucks was mounted with a machine gun. They made their way to the Kirwans' house. Young Jim was working in the field at the time. The Auxiliaries asked his father where Jim was and he told them that he was loading manure on a horse and cart. He was then ordered into the house, followed by two of the Auxiliaries. They asked him if there were any other Kirwan family members living in the village, and he replied 'No.' One of them then asked him for something to eat, and Kirwan proceeded to butter some bread and also gave him a cup of milk. They then said to the man that his son, Jim, was involved in the Kilroe ambush. Just then, a number of shots rang out. The father, unaware of the significance of the shots, told the Auxiliaries that his son had been working in the fields the day of the ambush and he could get at least forty witnesses to this fact. They then let him go. Mr Kirwan left the house and walked along the road towards the field where his son was working and met a number of Auxiliaries returning. One of them told him that his son had been shot as he tried to escape. In a panic, Kirwan ran to the field. The first thing he saw was the horse shot dead under the cart and about fifteen feet from the animal lay the body of his son. Kirwan began shouting for help. Neighbours arrived and took young Jim's remains home on the cart.

Three other men were also shot and wounded that day and a number of dwellings burned. The British had exacted a terrible retribution against people who had played no part in the ambush.[4]

In Galway city people were being stopped and questioned by the military. Some were told, 'We are after the Headford bucks' – this could indicate that they had an idea that men who carried out the ambush were from the Galway area. This was accompanied by bomb attacks on premises at night, one of the targets being Mahon's Hotel in Forster Street.[5] A number of people were arrested and taken to Renmore Barracks to face court martial. One was a woman, Alice Cashel, acting chairperson of Galway County Council. She was accused of having seditious documents with Dáil Éireann as the heading on the papers. Before passing sentence, the judge asked if she had anything to say. She replied:

> While not recognising the court, I wish to make a brief state-
> ment so that the stand I take may be quite understood. I hold
> that I would be justified in having documents in my possession.
> And acting upon any instructions that might be issued to me

being acting-chairman of Galway County Council – a council pledged to Dáil Éireann – the only government which I and they recognise, namely, the Government of the Irish Republic.[6]

On the night of 6 February 1921, a number of houses in Castlegar were attacked and burned. The home of the Mulryan family was destroyed by fire, as were the dwellings belonging to Thomas Fallon and Luke Ryan. Martin Coyne and his family were forced out of their home in Claregalway and forced to watch it burn, along with all their belongings. The Auxiliaries made no secret that this was in retaliation for the Kilroe ambush.[7]

The following Friday night the farm of Thomas Duggan in Rosshill was attacked. Both he and his wife awoke to loud banging and upon investigation were confronted by six armed men, who ordered them out of the house. They then set it alight. The gunmen then turned their attention on the barn and stables and set them on fire as Duggan set free his team of horses. Mrs Duggan made her way to a neighbour's house and spotted two military lorries at the end of the boreen. Saturday morning revealed the heads of some forty hens around the destroyed farmyard. The carcasses had been taken away.[8]

A week later, on Saturday night, houses in Dunmore were targeted and bombs were thrown through the windows as people slept. Shots were also discharged wildly in the town, causing widespread panic. The following morning the Auxiliaries held up and searched people making their way to Sunday mass. Similar events were experienced in Glenamaddy, where a Lewis gun was trained on people as they left mass. The following slogan was painted on the gable end of a shop: 'If one R.I.C. man is shot here, then up goes the town – God save the King.'[9]

By this time there were 100 prisoners being held in the Town Hall internment camp. They were cut off from freedom by high-wire fencing and barbed wire entanglements. Local children would often throw apples and such over the fence to the prisoners. St Patrick's Day was celebrated with a host of national songs from the many prisoners now being held there.[10]

Meanwhile, across the river, Galway Jail was now under the command of Pat Margetts. He was appointed shortly after the incident at Eyre Square, when his men had opened fire on the Crossley Tender. By this period, he had become acquainted with several leading republicans, including Seán Broderick, Stephen Jordan, George Nicholls and Professor Liam O'Brien of University College Galway. The prisoners at the jail were well treated and catered for – their friends were allowed to bring in food to them while they were awaiting trial. For the most part, the military guards were on friendly terms with the prisoners, and contrary to all regulations they supplied cigarettes and passed on letters and parcels to the inmates. It was an easy tour of duty at the jail, and when the main gate was locked up for the night, the sentries usually retired. Galway Jail had the distinction of housing the first priest arrested and charged with the possession of arms and ammunition during the troubles. He was Fr Morley, a curate from Headford. His trial took place in Renmore Barracks and he was sentenced to nine months' hard labour. While Margetts was in charge, both sides respected each other within the confines of the jail. In fact, conditions were such that he felt confident enough to leave the prison every night secure in the knowledge that all would be well when he returned in the morning.

A number of Auxiliaries were also held in Galway Jail, awaiting a military court martial for robbery and looting around the city. Margetts, who had once said that the Black and Tans were guilty of everything they were accused of and more, acted as escort to the prisoners when the evidence was produced and was shocked by the outcome. The court martial was a sham: the Auxiliaries were found not guilty and, to make matters worse, some were later promoted.[11]

21

Clifden Attacked

On the morning of 14 March 1921, Thomas Whelan of Sky Road, Clifden, was hanged in Mountjoy Jail, having been incorrectly found guilty of the killing of Captain G. T. Baggallay at 119 Lower Baggot Street on 21 November 1920. He was accused of being part of the Michael Collins 'hit squad' that eliminated most of the Dublin Castle 'Cairo Gang' of British intelligence officers determined to defeat the IRA.[1] Five other suspected IRA men were also hanged that morning.

Whelan was born in 1899 and was one of fourteen children. He joined a local Sinn Féin club while still in his teens. In 1918 he moved to Dublin, where he had secured work with the Midland and Great Western Railway Company in Broadstone Station. While in Dublin he joined C Company, Dublin Brigade IRA. He was arrested in January 1921 and faced trial on 1 February, where he pleaded not guilty. Although a British Army officer and soldier gave damning evidence against him, the truth of this was called into question.[2] The British officer stated that he was in his room shaving when he was confronted by two armed men, whom he identified as J. Boyce and Thomas Whelan. Both he and his housemaid were held in the bathroom while a number of other men went to Baggallay's room and shot him dead. The housemaid was not called to give evidence. As the men left the building they were observed by a soldier who had stopped on his motorcycle when he heard the shots. From this group, he identified M. J. Tobin, J. MacNamara and Thomas Whelan. However, there were a number of defence witnesses called who gave evidence that Whelan could not have been part of the gang that killed Baggallay. His landlady said that he went to 9 a.m. mass that morning and returned for his breakfast at 10 a.m. A lady living in the same street stated that she had seen him at mass. Another witness stated that he met the accused on Ringsend Bridge and had a conversation with him.

Despite the doubts about the evidence against Whelan, he was sentenced to death. The others, Boyce, MacNamara and Tobin, were all found not guilty.[3] The evidence given by the witnesses confirming Tommy Whelan's alibi was even published in the newspapers, and the public were outraged, but the authorities would not entertain the idea of his innocence.[4]

Monsignor Patrick MacAlpine from Clifden tried to undo the injustice that was to be carried out and approached the lord lieutenant, but his appeals fell on deaf ears. Whelan's mother travelled to Dublin to be close to her son during his final days. The day before the hangings took place there were huge protests outside Mountjoy Jail. Mrs Whelan and two other women – it was suggested that one of them was a girlfriend – went to see the prisoner for the last time that day. He assured them that he had no fear and that he was prepared to meet God a completely innocent man. He also asked his mother to forgive those who were responsible for his death, as he forgave all his enemies. When Mrs Whelan emerged from the prison, she told reporters, 'When all is over I will return to my native Clifden and never see Dublin again. Perhaps it would have been far better if poor Tom had never seen it … It is hard to think that he should have to make the supreme sacrifice for a crime that he had neither knowledge of, hand, act, nor part in, but God's Holy Will be done.'[5]

It was reported that Whelan sang 'The Shawl of Galway Grey' on the night before his execution. On the morning of his death he was still protesting his innocence. There were five other men hanged with him that morning, accused of separate killings: Patrick Moran, Thomas Bryan, Patrick Doyle, Frank Flood and Bernard Ryan. It was estimated that some 40,000 people gathered outside Mountjoy on that cold, dark morning, many in silent prayer. The Irish Transport and General Workers' Union called for all work to cease that day. Businesses throughout Dublin and Clifden closed that morning and there was a general atmosphere of grief across Ireland.[6] It was stated that 'no sound of human activity disturbed the solemn silence that hung heavily over the entire city'. By 8 a.m. all the executions had taken place and some twenty minutes later the crowd were informed by a notice placed on the prison gate.[7]

A few hours before his execution, Whelan wrote a letter

to the Lord Mayor of Dublin, in which he stated, 'We are always ready like Irishmen to die for our old cause. I am in the best of spirits now as always. An Irishman's honour is a great pledge, so like men, we shall meet our doom in the morning.' He also thanked him for the kindness shown to his mother throughout the ordeal. In a letter to the press following the execution, Mrs Whelan said that she earnestly hoped that before she died she would see Ireland free of courts martial and British law. She hoped that 'before many years, not years, but months, not months but weeks, that the sun of freedom will shine on our land'.

The local IRA in Clifden decided to exact revenge for the hanging of Thomas Whelan. Their policy was now 'two for one' – for every one of their men killed, they were going to kill two RIC or military men. Two nights later, on 16 March 1921, an RIC patrol consisting of four armed constables set out from their barracks on Main Street. The patrol split into pairs before reaching Market Street. One pair, Charles Reynolds and Thomas Sweeney, were approached by three or four men wearing trench coats. The constables did not suspect anything. Moments later the IRA men began shooting, killing Reynolds and mortally wounding Sweeney. The other two constables, who were ahead of their comrades, ran to the Market House for cover upon hearing the shots. The IRA men then grabbed the arms from the constables they had shot and began firing at the police running for cover, before making their escape. The police later reported that they were also fired on from another location near the railway station.

When the shooting stopped, the constables ran to the barracks for assistance, and, led by the chief constable, they recovered the body of Reynolds and a badly wounded Sweeney. Monsignor MacAlpine was summoned to attend to the spiritual needs of the wounded man and to administer the last rites to Constable Reynolds. He then returned to his home in the sincere hope that there would be no reprisals. Sweeney was first taken to the Workhouse Hospital and then transferred to St Brides Home in Galway, where he died two days later.

There was a genuine fear that the Clifden barracks would be attacked that night also, so the men within tried to contact Galway city for support. The telegraph wires had been cut, but it seems that a message was sent from the Marconi station outside Clifden to London, which was then relayed back to the police in Galway city, who immediately assembled their forces and organised transport. People in Clifden were totally unaware of the gathering storm as the Tans and Auxiliaries assembled at Galway Railway Station.[8]

A short time later, during the early hours of the morning, St Patrick's Day, some thirty Black and Tans and other armed men left Galway by 'special' train for Clifden, with murder and vengeance on their minds.[9] The military also sent a party of troops and Auxiliaries by road. Upon arriving in Clifden, the Tans immediately set out to attack the houses of known nationalists. However, these men had made their escape through the rear of the houses before the Tans got to them. The Tans began drinking and looting as they searched for republicans, and people fled from their homes as word spread that the Tans were on the rampage. Valuables and money were stolen and some fourteen houses were set alight.

One of the targets was MacDonnell's Hotel on Main Street. The owner was Alex MacDonnell. His son, John, was confronted by four or five Tans and two RIC men as he made his way to the burning hotel. They shot him dead and left his blood-covered body lying on the road. A former Connaught Ranger, he was a veteran of the Great War, in which he had fought with true courage and was promoted to sergeant major.

The home of Thomas Whelan was also targeted. His brothers had escaped and only his father, grandparents and young children were in the house at the time. His mother was still in Dublin, traumatised by the hanging of her son. As daylight approached, the Auxiliaries arrived in the deserted, burning town. Monsignor MacAlpine was awakened at about 6 a.m. that morning by a man banging on his door, calling out to him that the town was ablaze.[10] MacAlpine made his way into the town and was shocked at the sight before him: houses were burning and uniformed soldiers were firing shots through windows and into the air. One of the Tans approached him and asked what he was doing there. Monsignor MacAlpine replied, 'This is sad work on such a feast day.' The Tan then said, 'You get away out of here, we do not want your sort here.' Monsignor MacAlpine then went to the barracks and while he was speaking with one of the policemen, the Tan re-appeared. He had followed him to the barracks and this time he threatened him, saying, 'I will give you while I am counting four, and if you are not out of it by that time, you will never be out of it,' and pointed his gun at the priest's chest. One of the Irish policemen interfered and stopped the Tan from carrying out his threat.[11]

The fire attacks continued and in some places livestock were burned to death as outhouses were set alight. Some people sought refuge in the workhouse and convent, and as the morning wore on many were reassured by the crown forces that it was safe to return home. At about 8 a.m. Peter Clancy, who was looking after his brother's pub on Main Street, was shot in the head and neck. The Tans had come to the pub looking for more drink. One of them called Clancy outside to the yard, where he was knocked to the ground and shot three times; the bullets passed through his jaw, mouth and neck. Incredibly, he survived, and was removed to hospital in Galway where he eventually recovered, but he bore the scars for the remainder of his life.

St Patrick's Day 1921 turned out to be the worst day in the history of Clifden. The Tans and Auxiliaries made their way back to Galway and people began to venture into the streets and assess the damage. Sixteen houses were burned out by the Tans, other buildings were damaged and the windows of many homes had been shattered by bullets. Some 300 people sought refuge in the workhouse; many had lost all their possessions, but took comfort in the fact that they had not lost their lives. Monsignor MacAlpine, when interviewed later, said that he could only describe it as 'hell let loose'.[12]

There was genuine sympathy displayed by the people of the

town when the bodies of the two constables, Charles Reynolds and Thomas Sweeney, were being taken to the railway station and home for burial, the former to Kenagh, County Longford, and the latter to Aughrim, County Galway. Both men had been well liked within the community.[13]

22

Terror on Both Sides

On 24 March 1921, Commandant Louis D'Arcy of the Headford IRA Battalion was captured with a colleague at the Oranmore Railway Station. Both of them were taken to the local police barracks in the village, where they were questioned and tortured. The following morning, D'Arcy was placed in a Crossley Tender, supposedly to be taken to Galway Jail. However, once outside the village, he was tied to the back of the vehicle and dragged along the road to a field where the Oranmore Lodge is located today. A seven-year-old girl was picking potatoes in the field and ran to a wall. Looking over, she witnessed D'Arcy, bloody and battered, being lifted into the back of the lorry. He was then taken to the scene of the Merlin Park ambush in August of the previous year. His battered body was untied and the Tans shot him a number of times, putting him out of his agony. As was normal routine, it was later stated by Dublin Castle that he was shot while trying to escape.[1]

D'Arcy and a colleague, John Geoghegan, had been watched for some time by the Tans. Geoghegan was taken from his home in Moycullen and shot dead by the Tans, who placed a note on his body: 'Yours faithfully, Michael Collins.'[2] D'Arcy had been on his way to meet Collins and had taken great care, staying at three safe houses during the previous twenty-four hours. The first was the home of Pat Kavanagh, who brought him to a family named Glynn in Lydican. From there he moved to the Quinn home a few miles from Oranmore. His colleague had made his own way to Oranmore. Early the following morning, D'Arcy had been taken by sidecar to Oranmore, where his fate awaited him. It was evident that someone had informed on him, and many years later it was suggested that a former girlfriend had told the authorities where they would find him.[3]

The following night, 25 March 1921, St Patrick's Hall in Prospect Hill was attacked and burned by the Tans. This was an obvious target, given that it was the Sinn Féin Hall at the time and was being used for meetings and training. It was a detached four-storey building, and was formerly known as Foresters' Hall.[4] By the time of the troubles it was called the Thomas Ashe Sinn Féin Hall. There was a large basement where the Volunteers trained with wooden guns twice weekly. It was also used for drilling and lectures on various Irish subjects. Training for street fighting was also part of the programme.[5] Cumann na mBan had one of the top rooms, while the Galway branch of the Irish Transport and General Workers' Union occupied the ground floor. The premises were also used as a courthouse from time to time. The Tans doused the building with petrol and set it alight. The fire was so intense that some roofs of the thatched houses on the opposite side of the road began to catch fire and it took a concerted effort on the part of the neighbours to prevent the entire street from being destroyed. The Tans simply watched in amusement as people battled to save their homes.[6]

One has to question the wisdom of the senior military officers. On 1 April General Tudor, Chief of Police in Ireland, paid an overnight visit to Galway in the company of other senior military personnel. The following morning he inspected D Company of the RIC and Auxiliaries stationed at Lenaboy. He addressed the RIC first and congratulated them on the determined stand they had taken in lifting the reign of terror by gunmen all over the county, adding, 'I assure you that you have my fullest support.' Having inspected the Auxiliaries, he told them that it gave him great pleasure to hear of the excellent discipline they displayed. He also mentioned the Kilroe ambush, but made no mention of the murders carried out in reprisal.[7] Nor did he mention the murder that week of thirty-year-old Patrick Cloonan, whose half-naked body was found on the seashore at Maree. Cloonan had been taken from the home of Laurence Donoghoe to the shore the previous night by armed men, where he had been shot through the heart. He was a known member of Sinn Féin.[8] Tudor's address to his men would not help matters: he was more or less giving them a licence to do as they wished by assuring them of his full support.

The night that Tudor left Galway, a fifty-eight-year-old ex-British soldier was taken from his home near Kinvara by the IRA. His body was discovered the following day. He had been shot. A note was attached to his body stating, 'Convicted spy; tried, convicted and executed – IRA.'[9] Just over a week later, the IRA shot two constables, Michael Dunne and Simon Brennan, in an ambush near Milltown. Both men survived, but the shootings unnerved the other constables in the area – no area seemed safe in Galway city or county.[10]

On the night of 29 June, four armed Auxiliaries, dressed partially in uniform, broke through the front door of Flannery's house and business premises in Milltown. They quickly made their way upstairs and pulled Denis Flannery out of bed. They threw him down the stairs, then dragged him out into the street, where they continued to beat him. They demanded to know the whereabouts of his brother, but Flannery either did not know or would not tell them. The gunmen then proceeded to smash a number of windows.[11]

Attacks such as this only made matters worse. Another ambush took place at Milltown on the night of 27 July 1921, in which two policemen were shot dead – Sergeant Murren and Constable Day. They were part of a patrol that was ambushed. Two other constables made it back to the barracks uninjured. It was believed that this attack was carried out with the support of ex-army soldiers.[12]

The police and military were in an almost constant state of alert, not just in the city, but because of the amount of emergency calls from around the county. Connemara was not a popular area for them to have to travel through. Vehicles were scarce on the roads and could be seen from miles away in certain areas of this wild and rugged landscape. It was always more dangerous in mountainous regions, as all the roads were overlooked, creating an ideal location for snipers.

On 6 April a party of six police was ambushed at Screebe near Maam in Connemara. The sergeant and one of the constables were cycling about ten metres ahead of the others when the shooting started. Both men jumped from their bikes and dived for cover, rolling into a ditch and straight into the hands of the IRA. The two policemen were immediately disarmed and held captive. The other constables moved forward and returned fire. During the exchange of fire, one of the police was severely wounded, forcing his comrades back. There were reprisals that night, with a number of houses being burned in the area of the ambush.[13]

Just over two weeks later, on 23 April, an eleven-hour gun battle took place between police and republicans at Kilmilkin, on the Leenane Road, about five miles from Maam. A fourteen-man police patrol left Oughterard at 3 p.m. by lorry. They placed bicycles in the back of the vehicle and switched to the bicycles near Leenane to try to avoid being detected. Their mission was to raid the home of Padraic O'Maille, a member of Dáil Éireann for Connemara, which a flying column of the IRA was believed to be using as a base. The police cycled about twenty metres apart and then turned off the road, as the house was situated about 250 metres back from it. The area behind the house was mountainous and as they approached they noticed smoke coming from the chimney and the door opening and then closing. Moments later, shots rang out, and the sergeant and leading policemen dashed for cover. Gunmen ran from the house and took up position in the hills to the rear of the dwelling. A steady gunfight ensued, which went on for hours, during which two constables – Sergeant Hanley and Constable Ruttledge – were wounded and Constable John Boylan was shot dead. Hanley was wounded twice while trying to gain better cover and was forced to lie still as bullets whizzed about him. Ruttledge, who was lying in a small drain and almost immersed in water, observed a motor car driving towards the scene and made a dash towards the vehicle. He jumped on to the running board of the car and ordered the shocked driver to 'drive like hell for Maam'. As the car took off at speed one of the IRA men, realising that the policeman was getting away, began firing at the vehicle and its outside passenger, who was about a half mile from the scene of the gun battle when he was hit. However, he still managed to reach his destination, and notified the military in Galway.

Nevertheless, the IRA held the high ground and made full use of it. One constable later reported that the policemen were assisted by showers of sleet and rain. He said that all the police were pinned to the ground as there was very little cover. In his report, the policeman stated:

> The bullets whizzed all around us like hailstones and ploughed through the bog and the road while we lay there inactive, except for an occasional opportunity to fire, knowing that if night came without relief we were doomed. When the rain and hail storm passed, the concentrated fire ceased. Not a puff of smoke was to be seen on the hills to indicate the position of our attackers,

who then settled down to sniping until another shower or mist came to act as a natural smoke screen on the mountains over our heads.

Meanwhile, Fr Cunningham, the curate from Leenane, arrived to attend to the wounded, but was unable to reach the body of Constable Boylan because of the intense firing. Reinforcements consisting of seven lorry loads of police and Auxiliaries and an armoured car mounted with a Vickers machine gun were rushed to Connemara. By the time they reached the attack area, the main body of IRA men had already retreated across the hills towards Maamtrasna and Lough Mask. However, before leaving, they had positioned snipers in several positions in the hills who fired on the lorries and armoured car when they arrived. All were more or less pinned down until the firing stopped. The military gave it some time before venturing into open for fear of being shot. They then made a nervous search of the now-silent hills, but by this time the snipers had also retreated. Before leaving the area they searched O'Maille's house, where a number of female members of the family had remained under cover while the shooting was going on. In the outhouses they discovered a quantity of guns and ammunition and sleeping accommodation for about forty men. O'Maille's family was forced out of the house by the military and the building was then set on fire. A neighbour's house was also evacuated and burned.[14]

Some weeks later a six-man police patrol under Sergeant Rodgers was ambushed in Spiddal. It had just left the police barracks at 4 a.m., when it came under attack. The IRA members were concealed opposite the barracks in the old chapel yard and an adjacent building. As soon as the police were clear of the building, the gunmen opened fire. The police returned fire, by which time their comrades in the barracks began firing to give the police caught outside time to retreat to safety. The shooting lasted about ten minutes and no one was hit. It was later discovered that the road to Galway had been barricaded.[15]

The Tans became extremely active in Connemara after these attacks and would travel in groups as well as in Crossley Tenders. The IRA then began destroying bridges throughout the countryside. Most of this work was done manually, as there were not sufficient explosives to blow all of the bridges. One of the men involved in this work and in the Screebe ambush was George Staunton, a vice-commandant in the local IRA.[16]

On 29 April a twenty-six-year-old man was taken from his home at Kilroe near Headford. His mother was held at gunpoint and after a short time heard shots. The masked gunmen then left, and a few minutes later the woman found her son's body some twenty-five metres from the house. It was reported that the IRA carried out the attack, as they believed the man to be an informer. According to one witness called to give evidence during the inquiry, there was a note on his body which read, 'Reported informer; Convicted spy; Others beware IRA.' However, the note was not recovered, so there was no definite proof of why the man was killed, but it was mentioned that he was the fifth man to die since the Kilroe ambush.[17]

The following night, Saturday, the IRA entered Headford and began a sustained attack on the fortified police barracks. It was about 2.45 a.m. when the barracks was hit with a barrage of fire from various positions in the town. The attack began suddenly and police reacted in panic, rushing for their weapons. They had steel shutters on the windows with loopholes from which they could return fire. One attacker lobbed a grenade onto the roof, which, when it exploded, created a hole in the building, while gunfire at the rear severely damaged the door and windows. A deep trench had been cut across the Galway to Headford Road, the road between the town and Shrule was also barricaded, while other roads were blocked by trees to prevent reinforcements reaching the town.

The police in Headford were now isolated and there was a great sense of fear inside the barracks. The town echoed with the sound of gunfire and people remained in their homes. However, the barracks was very well fortified and the attack was called off after about two hours.[18]

The IRA was active again on Sunday evening when members ambushed a five-man motor police patrol on the Dunmore to Tuam road. The lorry ground to a halt quickly as the police ran for cover, before returning fire. The engagement lasted some twenty minutes and the IRA was forced to retreat as police reinforcements arrived from Dunmore.[19]

23

Terror in the Terrace

On 10 May 1921, IRA Volunteer James Folan was released from Galway Jail. He had served six months for being caught with seditious documents. Upon leaving prison, he was warned by one of the prison wardens not to stay at his home in O'Donoghoe's Terrace that night. He took this advice and made his way to a safe house.[1] Late that night a group of Tans arrived at his home. They banged on the door and it was opened by one of his brothers, Patrick. They were looking for James. When Patrick told them he was not at home, a search of the house and yard began. Two of his younger brothers, Christopher and Joseph, slept in a ground-floor bedroom. The Tans entered the room, lit a match and shot Christopher. They then left the room momentarily and upon returning shot Joseph as he held a lighted lamp, trying to support the body of his dead brother. Joseph was taken to hospital, where he later recovered. The Tans had made no attempt to question any of the brothers, who were completely innocent – this was simply murder.

The Tans then proceeded to 35 St Bridget's Terrace, where they demanded entry. The house was owned by Thomas

Carew and his wife, who had a young man, Hubert Tully, staying with them.[2] Tully was a foreman in Galway Railway Station, twenty-six years old, a native of County Roscommon and a contact of Seán Broderick. As with some other raids and shootings, it seems likely that informers must have passed along information on him to the Tans.[3] When Carew answered the door the Tans pushed past him, demanding to see Tully. Two then went to Tully's room and forced him down the stairs. Once they had him at the bottom of the stairs, they asked him if he was Hubert Tully. As soon as he replied in the affirmative, they shot him a number of times. He fell to the ground, but was still alive. His landlady pleaded with the Tans not to kill him, but they simply pushed her aside and pulled Tully up so that his head rested against the pillar of the staircase. Before leaving, they shot him through the head.[4]

Hubert Tully was a friendly young man and would join in the children's fun and games on his way home from work, as he had done that evening. But there had been an atmosphere of uneasiness about the street that day – the children who were playing had noticed Tans at the top of the road. One of the children, Kathleen Traynor, had an older brother, James, who was a member of the IRA. He had a narrow escape that night, as the Tans were also looking for him. Traynor owed his life to Constable Jack Kelly, who lived across the street. Earlier, he had called to the Traynor home and asked to see James. Kelly warned James not to stay at home that night and told him that the safest place for him was to spend the night in his attic. Of course, Traynor was a little suspicious at first, but after considering his options he decided to take up the policeman's offer. After their spree of raiding and killing that night, the Tans called at the home of Jack Kelly, who had no choice but to invite them in lest they become suspicious. They sat in his open kitchen and had a drink while James Traynor remained hidden and silent upstairs. While Traynor survived the Black and Tan war and the subsequent Civil War, he died shortly afterwards.[5]

On another occasion, IRA Brigadier Tom Powell (later Dr Powell of Abbeygate Street) from south Mayo used the home of P. J. and Mary Kennedy in 26 St Bridget's Terrace as a safe house. He had to share a bed with young Tommy Kennedy, a ten-year-old boy. One night the Auxiliaries arrived, but Powell had heard the Crossley Tender coming down the street and, taking no chances, he had grabbed his clothes and made his way out the back before they gained entrance to the house. As Powell made his escape over the old railway wall and through the railway tunnel, the military searched the house. In his urgency to escape, Powell had left his revolver under the pillow where he had been sleeping, but the Auxiliaries did not find it. Early the following morning, when Mary Kennedy went to her son's room, as she entered a shot rang out and a bullet struck the door beside her head. The child had found the gun and was playing with it when it discharged. It seems the bullet was left lodged in the door for many years, a reminder of those brutal times.[6]

The late Paddy O'Neill of Shantalla, and formerly of 27 St Bridget's Terrace, was interviewed in November 2005 at 101 years of age. During the interview, Paddy said that he never forgot that night, as he was awoken by the 'shots that sent [his] young friend Christy Folan to the grave'. He spoke of the terror in the terrace that night as the Tans shot Hubert Tully and went looking for other suspects. He also remembered standing at the corner of the street one night when three men passed by, walking towards Prospect Hill. In the semi-darkness he watched as they made their way to the home of an RIC constable there. O'Neill was unsure of exactly what happened, but he heard a shot and saw the men run back towards the terrace and turn down a nearby lane. Paddy and the others ran to their respective homes quickly, afraid to tell anyone what they had witnessed. The following day, they heard that the wife of the RIC constable had been shot. It seemed that the constable would not open the door at night to anyone unless he was sure who it was. If there was a knock on the door, he was in the habit of looking out through the letterbox. On that particular night, it was his wife that went to answer the door, and before opening the door she had done the same. She immediately received a gunshot wound to the head, which was intended for her husband – the gunman had the barrel of his weapon just outside the letterbox. The callers were obviously aware of the man's routine. Paddy said that the family left Galway shortly afterwards.[7]

Paddy also knew James Traynor and was a friend of his younger brothers. The family was never sure of the whereabouts of Traynor as he felt it was safer for them not to know. However, it later became common knowledge that he and some of his comrades had slept in the tombs in Forthill Cemetery from time to time. Very few people would venture into cemeteries at night, and that included military personnel. Leaving one man on sentry duty ensured a good night's sleep for the others. The local republicans knew Forthill well as most had family buried there, and there was always a group of them, which included Tom Courtney, willing to sleep with the dead. One night the sentry fell asleep and was awoken by the sound of a Crossley Tender making its way towards the cemetery. Those sleeping there made a quick dash over the back wall of the cemetery and all escaped.[8]

Three nights after the murders of Christopher Folan and Hubert Tully, two other men were shot in separate incidents and a third had a lucky escape. John Greene, who had served for four years with the British Army during the Great War, was lodging at Reilly's Hotel in Salthill. He was a native of Sligo and was studying engineering in University College Galway. Two other students, Patrick MacDonogh and Gerard Hanley, were sleeping in the same room. About an hour after they retired, they heard shots outside the hotel, and a few minutes later two men entered the room and spoke with them. They then fired a number of shots through the window and floor and left. A short time later, the students heard a voice from downstairs say, 'It's Greene we want.' The two gunmen returned and ordered Greene downstairs, not allowing him to get dressed.

Another man, James Egan, who was staying at the hotel that night, was also assaulted and was at the bottom of the stairs, covered in blood, being guarded by two other gunmen. Egan was from Tuam and was also a former soldier, but had since become the Health Insurance Agent for County Mayo. Egan had only just come to Galway that day to attend a funeral. As Greene was being taken downstairs, one of the gunmen shot him in the back. Egan later said that the bullet passed through the prisoner, exiting through his side. As they took Greene outside, he said to Egan, 'I am afraid we are done.' Hanley, who had also been ordered outside, made a dash for freedom and managed to get away. In the confusion, Greene also tried to escape, but was too weak to run.

Greene was taken down to the seashore, where the gunmen proceeded to assault him with a truncheon and revolver butts, beating him to the ground. A number of his fingers were broken and his head was cut. They asked him what he knew about Sinn Féin and accused him of receiving money from the republicans. He denied knowing anything about the republican movement. After a few minutes, a third gunman arrived, and told him to say his prayers as they were going to finish him off. He was then shot a second time. This bullet went through his neck without doing fatal damage. They stooped over him and one of them asked, 'Are you dead?' Greene lay perfectly still and, believing that he was dead, his assailants left the area. Greene hid in between the rocks on the beach for a while and then managed to struggle back to the hotel, where he was attended by a doctor a short time later.

James Egan was subjected to similar treatment. Every time the gunmen hit Egan, they would shout, 'Are you loyal now

– you Sinn Féiner?' He told them that he had nothing to do with Sinn Féin, saying that he had served in the British Army during the war, but they took no notice. They then marched him along the road towards the promenade and told him to walk into the sea. By now, Egan's face was a bloody mess, and his body ached from the beating. They began firing shots over him until he was almost neck-deep in the water. Then one of the attackers followed him and forced his head under the water. Egan was then dragged back to the shore, shoved up against a wall close to the beach and told to prepare for death. One of the men then asked, 'Are you ready?' He replied, 'Yes,' as death seemed the only way to end the agony. The Tan then shot him in the leg. One of the others then said, 'He missed you, but I won't,' and began battering Egan about the head and chest with his gun. The others then joined in the punishment. After they finished, they told Egan to get on home. He struggled back to the hotel, from where both he and Greene were taken to St Brides Home the following morning.

While recovering, both men made statements about their ordeal to Richard Cruise, who was by then a divisional inspector, and District Inspector MacGlynn. Both victims had no connection to the republican movement and were in fact war veterans, which MacGlynn took seriously. He was also surprised when Patrick MacDonogh came forward with evidence, as he was the son of an RIC county inspector. Within hours, two RIC constables, Richard Orford and John Murphy, were arrested and taken to Eglinton Street Barracks for questioning. Both had only been in the force a few weeks.

Most people in the town were on edge from the spate of attacks and were afraid to speak out and ask questions. The question whispered by many was how the police who attacked the two war veterans had been taken into custody so quickly, yet no one had been arrested for the murders of Folan and Tully?[9] The two constables faced trial in late July, where the full terror of their two victims was highlighted. Several police colleagues were called to give evidence, and all said that the accused men were perfectly sober that night. They also swore that the men were with them and that they had retired to bed by 10 p.m. that night, so they could not have been the men who attempted to murder the two ex-soldiers. After an address from the council for the prosecution, it was decided that summing up would be deliberated in private. Proceedings resumed a short time later with a verdict of not guilty on the charges brought against both policemen.[10]

24

Final Actions

During Christmas 1920, while still on the run, Seán Broderick received a message from John Spellman, who lived with his family in the gate lodge of Fermoyle in Connemara, saying that if he could make it to Derroe Cross arrangements could be made to secure a safe location for him to hide. Spellman was the caretaker of the main house at Fermoyle, and was sleeping there himself while the house was vacant. The Tans seemed to be everywhere and were stopping people and vehicles travelling on almost all roads. Broderick enlisted the help of Joe Togher, who provided a long canvas mail bag. Broderick got into the bag, which was then placed by Togher in the mail delivery van. Luckily, this was the Christmas period, so when the Tans stopped the van at Spiddal to search it and saw the number of parcels, they decided to wave it through. Once Broderick reached Derroe Cross and made his way to Fermoyle lodge, he was well received by John Spellman and was given a room in the big house itself in which to sleep.

Then, on the night of 6 January 1921, Tans entered the

lodge and made their way to the bedrooms. They had switched off the engine of the lorry and allowed it to roll down the incline on the road towards the house so as not to alert the occupants to their presence. The Spellman family was caught totally by surprise and interrogated as to the whereabouts of the Galway man on the run. When the Tans didn't get satisfactory answers, they began to ransack the place. John Spellman, in the main house, heard the noise and immediately woke Broderick, who climbed into the attic by means of a rope ladder, pulling it up after himself. Spellman grabbed Broderick's bedclothes, brought them to his own room and threw them onto the bed. He then turned Broderick's mattress upside down in case they checked to see if it was warm. He was just back in his own bed when the Tans broke into the house. They dragged Spellman out of bed and shoved the barrel of a gun into his mouth. He was told that he would have his brains blown out if he did not tell them where the Shinner was hiding out. They then proceeded to beat him up before apparently leaving. However, when Spellman went to Broderick's room to see if the Tans had discovered anything incriminating, two Tans were there waiting for him. Spellman began acting strangely and talking nonsense, in the hope that the Tans would think his actions were the result of the beating he had received. It was unclear how the Tans had known of Broderick's presence at the house.

Alternative accommodation was arranged for Broderick in a large cave near the village of Fermoyle. It had a wooden floor and was furnished with a bed and oil lamp. It was not accessible from the road and was supplied with food by trusted local people.[1]

These were hungry days for the men on the run, and some houseowners in Ballybane would leave their doors unlocked at night and food on the table. One man who availed himself of this hospitality was Jim Furey. He had worked as a mechanic in Ward's Garage near Eyre Square, but on the morning the Tans killed Seán Mulvoy and Seamus Quirke they had arrived at the garage to have routine repairs carried out on one of their trucks. In a fit of anger, Jim Furey had taken a sledgehammer to the engine and destroyed it. This action had forced him to go on the run, and he had been running ever since.

Castlegar, Rahoon and Menlo were other areas outside the city where republicans would not go hungry. There was one house in Kiloughter, the home of Mrs Mary Small, where they could always depend on a meal. It was said that she fed companies of IRA men. Her family also hid weapons in the thatched roof and survived a number of raids.[2] There were a number of safe houses in the city also, but as the war progressed, military raids intensified, forcing many republicans into the countryside.

Hubert Tully, through his job at Galway Railway Station, had been very important in getting arms to the IRA in Galway. Following his death, Tom Courtney became involved in carrying weapons between Dublin and Galway. During one of his journeys from Dublin he had a close encounter with death. On this occasion, he was carrying a timber suitcase full of small arms and Mills bombs. The normal method of ensuring that the weapons reached the IRA was to have a predetermined drop-off point along the railway line before the train reached Galway Station, as the military sometimes set up checkpoints there. Shortly after Courtney boarded the train, two armed Tans entered his carriage and sat down. They spoke to him, exchanging general conversation, and asked if he would play a game of cards to shorten the journey. Although nervous, he agreed, smiling in a bid to cover his concern and not draw too much attention to himself. There was no table in the carriage, and one of the Tans grabbed his suitcase from the seat, saying that they could use it as a table. The Tan commented that the case was very heavy, but Courtney kept his cool and told him that it was a case of snooker balls for the Temperance Club in Galway. The Tan did not pursue the matter and told his colleague to deal the cards.

Throughout the journey, Courtney continued to play cards and hold a conversation. The men were part of a group of Tans going to Galway and had not been there before. Courtney praised Galway and kept chatting with the pair as the train moved across the landscape. However, he missed his drop-off for the arms. As the train rushed towards Galway, he became concerned about the possibility of a military checkpoint at the station. There was an alternative plan in place, involving a girl who would pose as his wife, but Courtney was on his own until he was out of the station.

When the train reached the station, one of the Tans offered to carry his suitcase, commenting again on its weight. Courtney's worst fears were realised – there was a military checkpoint at the exit and people were being stopped and searched. Courtney made his way along the platform towards the checkpoint at the exit. It seemed a very long walk. Fortunately, he was not stopped, but waved through because of the company he was in. Outside, two IRA men watched almost in disbelief as Courtney, escorted by the Tans, one of them actually carrying the suitcase, emerged from the station. The Tans asked Courtney if he had far to go. He replied 'No', adding that his wife was collecting him, and smiled at the young woman sitting on the pony and trap close to the exit. She was also concerned and mystified upon seeing her 'husband' with the Tans. The Tans then walked with Courtney towards the woman and placed the suitcase on the trap. Before parting, they thanked him for his company and said that they had enjoyed the journey and the game of cards. Bidding him good evening, they turned and walked away towards Eyre Square to join their colleagues.

Courtney had another lucky escape some days later, when he encountered a military patrol, but a group of women gathered around him and enabled him to slip over a nearby wall. He landed in a bed of nettles and had to lie still and endure the pain and discomfort for a time, but this was presumably preferable to being shot.

Following these episodes, he was sent to the United States, where he spent his time fund-raising. He remained there until the signing of the Truce. If aspects of Tom Courtney's story seem familiar, this may be because many years later the author Walter Macken interviewed him about his experiences when writing *The Scorching Wind*, a novel covering the period of the Black and Tan war in Galway.[3]

Courtney's friend and comrade Joe Togher, of the 'steaming and opening department', was arrested and taken to Galway Jail at around this time, where he was interrogated by a Captain Harrison. The military seemed to have a lot of accurate information and Togher suspected it was the work of informers. While in custody, he was told that he was second in line to be shot after Frank Hardiman, another prominent republican. However, instead, he was released, but believed that this was a ploy so that he could then be shot. Togher immediately went on the run and helped form a new company. He was wounded during an ambush in Achill Island, but recovered quickly. He also organised the burning of military stores and kept the Lancers at Earls Island busy by taking shots at their barracks from across the river along the Dyke Road. One night he became trapped near the Franciscans' boathouse on the west bank of the River Corrib, but managed to escape across the river to a place called the Iodine. He had another narrow escape when he decided to go to his home to try to get a good night's sleep in a comfortable bed. The Auxiliaries arrived, but Togher escaped out through a back window. However, he left his revolver behind – his mother spotted it before she answered the banging on the door. Grabbing the weapon, she hid it in her undergarments before letting the Auxiliaries into the house. They questioned her regarding her son's whereabouts and searched the premises. Before leaving, they damaged much of the furniture and broke ornaments. It was clear that someone was informing the authorities about Togher's movements.[4]

On 15 May 1921 an ambush took place at Ballyturn House near Gort, which resulted in the deaths of District Inspector Cecil Blake, his wife, Eliza Blake, Captain Cornwallis and Lieutenant MacCreery of the 17th Lancers. There was one survivor – Mrs Graham Parry Gregory, widow of Robert Gregory of Coole Park, who had been killed in the Great War.

District Inspector Blake had been stationed in Gort since the end of 1920. Ballyturn House was the home of the Bagot family and was located about four and a half miles from Gort on the Kilbeacanty road. The group had spent a pleasant afternoon as guests of the Bagots and at about 8.45 p.m. they had decided to leave. Hidden in the trees and bushes on both sides of the driveway were members of the IRA, who had also taken over the gate lodge near the entrance. As the motor car approached the closed gate, an unsuspecting Captain Cornwallis got out of the vehicle to open it. One of the IRA men shouted, 'Hands up!' and Cornwallis ran for cover behind the estate wall and began firing his revolver. Although he was protected from the men firing from the bushes, he was exposed to fire from the gate lodge, and he was shot dead by one of the men in that position. For a few minutes all hell broke loose and bullets shattered the windscreen of the car as the remaining occupants struggled out of the vehicle. Blake was already wounded and made an attempt to return fire, but the gun fell from his hand as the shooting continued. His wife clung to him, which sealed her fate. Lieutenant MacCreery was also hit a number of times and died almost immediately. Mrs Gregory, who had also got out of the car, made her way to the rear of the vehicle and kept low to the ground. When the firing ceased a man armed with a rifle walked up to her and led her back towards the house. The bodies of her four companions lay sprawled close to the car. It had all happened so fast that she was in shock, but as she got closer to the house the realisation of what had just taken place hit her and she ran in terror to the Bagots, who had come out to investigate. They had approached the ambush area, but were ordered back by the gunmen. However, one of their daughters had mounted a pony and trap and made her way to Gort via another route to raise the alarm. A party of police and military rushed to the scene of the ambush, but as they arrived a shot rang out from the shrubbery, mortally wounding one of them, Constable Kearney.[5] He was taken to St Brides Home in Galway where he later died – the fiftieth member of the force to be killed in an ambush.

The bodies of the ambush victims were taken to Renmore Barracks, where they were draped in the Union Jack. District Inspector Blake and his wife were buried in the New Cemetery, Galway, while the remains of Captain Cornwallis and Lieutenant MacCreery were taken home to England.[6] Some of the IRA men who took part in this ambush were Pat Houlihan, John Coen, Dan Ryan, Pat Glynn, Michael Kelly and Joseph Stanford. One of the men later stated that the reason that they had shouted 'Hands up!' was to give the soldiers time to consider the women's safety, but when Cornwallis began shooting, they returned fire. He also stated that Blake had built up a bad reputation in the area and his wife also carried a gun. It seems that she had threatened some people, saying that if anything happened to her husband, she would have Gort burned.[7]

The day before the Ballyturn ambush another woman, a Miss Barrington, had been killed under similar circumstances along with Major Henry Briggs, a district inspector with the Auxiliaries, near Newport in County Tipperary. The deaths of women led to much criticism of the republican movement by the authorities. This was answered strongly by a report in the *Irish Bulletin*:

> A state of war exists in Ireland. The British Government have formally declared it to exist, and have formally placed their troops on active service. British officers engaged in this war have no right to go about accompanied by ladies and expect immunity on that account. If they permit ladies to accompany them they are directly responsible for any harm that may unhappily befall them in the event of an attack. This is the rule in all wars.[8]

Before the military arrived at Ballyturn, a notice had been handed into the Bagots, stating that if there were any reprisals, the IRA would return and burn the house. However, there were reprisals and many people fled in terror that night. One witness said the horizon was fringed with flames as houses were burned in the area. A number of houses were damaged in Gort and a granary and an attached building were burnt to the ground. Curfew was imposed on the town and all business premises were ordered to close until further notice.

Another ambush took place almost a month later on the road between Mountbellew and Moylough. It began with an individual attack on Constable Patrick Nealon as he approached his home in Moylough in the company of his wife, three children and another lady. Just as he was about to turn the key in the door, two young men rode up on bicycles from Moylough. They quickly dismounted, drew revolvers and fired on the constable, who dived for cover. He then got to his feet and ran across a nearby field as the women and children became hysterical, attempting to stop the attackers from getting off any more shots. However, they did manage to wound him in the hand and then made their escape on the bikes.

Later that night two lorries and a car full of police and Auxiliaries travelled to Moylough to investigate the incident and to support the police there. Before they reached their destination, they were ambushed about halfway between Mountbellew and Moylough. The lorries and car ground to a halt and the military ran for cover along the roadside. Although they were well armed, it was difficult for them to return fire as to do so they had to raise their heads above the mounds of earth behind which they sheltered. The gunfight went on for about an hour and a half, during which time one of the policemen was wounded. This ambush was obviously well planned: the attack on the policeman was to draw the military into the area and the IRA had trenches dug in the fields so that during any retreat they would not have to expose themselves to any enemy fire.[9]

In June a large number of compensation cases were settled in the Galway Quarterly Sessions. Claims were made by people who had family members killed by the police and military. Others looked for compensation for loss of earnings due to attacks by police and for the loss of property when houses, businesses and haggards were burned. Celia Collins received £400 for the shooting of her son; other members of his family also received compensation. Sarah Hoade was awarded £650 for the shooting of her brother. (Both men had been shot after the Kilroe ambush.) John Kirwan received £400 for the loss of his son. The amount awarded totalled £200,000 at these hearings alone, and there were many more cases to be placed before the courts over the coming year.[10]

The military and the police were also submitting claims in the courts. The Auxiliaries wounded in the Kilroe ambush were awarded £12,000 between them. While the government may have been taking little notice of the mounting dead on both sides, compensation claims were certainly hitting the government coffers.[11]

The destruction continued on both sides. The Athenry tennis and cricket grounds were destroyed and the pavilion burned to the ground. In the burned-out debris of the building, police discovered the unrecognisable charred remains of a body. Petrol cans were found close to it, but it was not known if this was the person who started the fire.[12]

On 11 July a six-man patrol of police was ambushed near Kilchreest, Loughrea. It was believed that about forty men took part in the attack, which left one policeman seriously wounded.[13] This was the last engagement of the War of Independence in Galway.

25

The Dawn of Freedom

On 25 May 1921 several hundred IRA members had occupied and burned down the Customs House in Dublin (the centre of Irish local government records). While intended to show the untenability of British rule in Ireland, the ensuing battle had resulted in the deaths of five Volunteers and the capture of eighty. Michael Collins viewed this as a disaster. While there was no let-up in IRA activity afterwards, Collins believed that by June he would only be able to carry on the war for three more weeks.

A truce had been in the minds of politicians for some time. Lloyd George and the British government had come under strong pressure to resolve the Irish question, particularly from the United States. Winston Churchill was pushing for a truce. There were a number of others pursuing a peace process, among them Andy Cope, the under-secretary for Ireland, who worked tirelessly for a solution. Once Lloyd George removed his previous condition of a surrender of arms, the terms of a truce were agreed upon in the Mansion House, Dublin, by General Nevil Macready, commander-in-chief of the British forces in Ireland, and his aide Colonel Brind on the British side, and Robert Barton, minister for economics in the first Dáil, and Éamonn Duggan, another member of the first Dáil.[1] De Valera and Lloyd George had ultimately agreed to a truce that was intended to end the fighting and lay the ground for detailed negotiations. Once the Truce was signed on 8 July, de Valera indicated his willingness by telegram to meet with Lloyd George in London on 14 July. He was accompanied by Austin Stack, Arthur Griffith, Erskine Childers, Count Plunkett and Robert Barton. Sir James Craig represented the unionist interest. While this was in a sense the beginning of negotiations, it was clear even at this early stage, that partition was probably the best solution that could be achieved at this point in time.[2]

At 9 p.m. on the night of 11 July 1921, news of the Truce reached Galway. It came suddenly and dramatically and was displayed on the screen of the Empire cinema, interrupting the film. There was a pause of silence at first as the audience studied the announcement, followed by tumultuous applause as realisation that there was a ceasefire set in. As news of the Truce spread, people in the streets made their way to the railway station to await the mail train carrying the all-important newspapers. However, the papers were devoid of any information and an air of disappointment spread over the area as people began to doubt the authenticity of the news. This was followed by a rush on the offices of the *Connacht Tribune* newspaper. The windows were ablaze with light – printing presses buzzed and rattled as messages were coming through from Dublin and London at lightning speed. Word from those inside was that the news was correct – there was a ceasefire.

There was great rejoicing as people made their way home to rest and await the morning papers. Bonfires on the hills throughout Connacht signalled an end to the fighting. People were reminded of the last time that fires lit up the hills of Connacht, with the arrival of the 'Apostles of Freedom' in January 1919. Many families thought of their lost loved ones who had sacrificed their lives for this day.

The Truce was strictly observed throughout the county. Five lorry loads of Auxiliaries who were searching the Connemara mountains for IRA members returned to Lenaboy without firing a shot. There was a noticeable lack of police or military presence everywhere. All restrictions on markets and public meetings were lifted. Curfews ended. Alderman Michael Staines, TD, arrived in Galway from Dublin to act as liaison officer for the IRA. The men who were on the run returned to their homes amid great relief and joy.[3]

Although the Truce held, violence was not far away and could re-erupt given the right circumstances. On the Sunday night of 2 October 1921, a ceilidh was held in the Town Hall in Galway in aid of the Republican Prisoners' Dependants Fund. A huge crowd attended and no one was to be refused admission once he or she had paid. It seems that trouble broke out after some Auxiliaries attempted to attend the event without paying. The Auxiliaries said that they were held up and searched by republican police in the vicinity of the Town

Hall. A fight ensued and it was only when the windows of the hall were shattered by gunshots that the people attending the dance became aware that there was trouble. People threw themselves to the floor as the indiscriminate shooting continued for a few minutes. Members of the republican police tried to restore order, telling people that they had the situation under control. They said that the shots were blanks, but everyone knew that this was not the case. It was ten or fifteen minutes before it was realised that one soldier had been killed and a constable wounded. The soldier, Lieutenant Souchon of the 17th Lancers, was being driven past the Town Hall when the shooting started. Bullets had struck the car and the driver, Constable Barnes, who managed nevertheless to continue his journey to the military post at Earls Island. It was only when he arrived there that he realised that Lieutenant Souchon was dead in the back seat of the car – he had been killed instantly. Constable Barnes had been shot through the abdomen and was taken to St Brides Hospital, where he later recovered. Once news broke that a soldier had been killed, the ceilidh concluded and people began making their way home quietly. Both sides denied shooting the soldier and policeman. When the military arrived, soldiers moved to surround the Town Hall. As they approached a shot was fired from a side window. They took cover and returned fire. After a few minutes, they entered the building.

It was later alleged by a policeman that he entered the Town Hall after the shooting and was confronted by a man carrying a Webley revolver. He said that he disarmed the man but never asked him his name. He also stated that the revolver had been discharged twice. One of the Auxiliaries said the shots came from the windows of the Town Hall, which seems likely given that the people attending the dance dived for cover when the initial shots were fired. Another civilian witness said that a number of Auxiliaries arrived and attempted to gain admittance without paying. They were asked to leave and remained at the entrance for a few minutes. He said that a short time later a man with his face all bloody came into the hall and said that he had been beaten by the Auxiliaries. It was after this incident that the shooting started. There was the possibility that the IRA had fired on the car as it passed the building, but many people believed that the men were shot by accident as they were simply passing at the time and had not been involved in the incident outside the hall.

Whatever happened, Lieutenant Souchon became the last victim of the War of Independence in Galway. His remains were taken to Renmore Barracks en route to his home town in Surrey for burial. The people of the town showed great respect as the officer's remains were being taken to Renmore, with some shop shutters being pulled down.[4]

On the morning of 23 November, the Republican prisoners in Galway Jail barricaded themselves into the northern wing. Six wardens were taken prisoner by the inmates and fires were set. News of the protest sent out alarm bells and police and Auxiliaries were rushed to the jail. People gathered in the vicinity, watching the smoke as it rose above the prison walls.

The outbreak of the protest was a direct result of the

treatment of Diarmuid Crowley, a republican judge who had been in custody since the previous January. Crowley had been ill for some time, and he and some of the others felt that the prison doctor was not performing his duty as he should have done and was prejudiced against Crowley. The issue had been raised with the governor of the jail and visiting justices, but it had not been resolved. Thus the prisoners took matters into their own hands. Early on the Wednesday morning they had broken into the paint shed and gathered any inflammable substances. They had then removed their bedding, covers and clothes, placed them in one of the halls on the ground floor of the southern wing and set them alight. A fire was also started in the northern wing, where the punishment cells had been broken into and everything that could be burned was torched. The wooden sections of the staircases in both wings of the prison were also on fire as the prisoners sang the 'Soldiers' Song' with great satisfaction. Along with the Auxiliaries, police and troops from Renmore Barracks and Earls Island rushed to the scene. There was a brief but somewhat bloody encounter as the military and police tried to recapture the prison and there were a number of injuries on both sides. The fires were brought under control and order was restored. Crowley was removed by ambulance to Galway Railway Station and from there sent to Mountjoy Jail in Dublin.[5]

There were calls from the public to release the prisoners and restore goodwill. The House of Commons had given Lloyd George a 'sweeping majority' to bring about peace in Ireland. The editor of the *Connacht Tribune* said the only real way of achieving this was to release all political prisoners. If the British government desired peace, he said, then it should take the steps to ensure that peace prevailed. He went on to say that the government, which had seldom done anything graciously or generously in Ireland, had again lived up to its reputation by keeping these men interned. Hundreds of Galway men, he added, were behind barbed wire, arrested without charge, imprisoned without charge, and it was the same across the country. The Truce would be further strengthened, he argued, if these men were to be released. This gesture would be a tangible and practical token in which all-round sanity and goodwill would prevail. It would also lessen the danger of violence and help stabilise the uneasy peace that their detention provoked.[6]

On 10 December the first group of the Galway prisoners held in Ballykinlar Internment Camp arrived home by train. They included Martin Crowe, Frank Henry, Patrick O'Connor, Peter Flaherty, James Curran, Michael Ward and John Hosty. They had all been arrested at the same time and had spent thirteen months in the prison camp. Conditions there had initially left much to be desired and the food, it was said, was not fit for human consumption. Food parcels from home supplemented the men's diet – they shared their supplies whenever necessary so that no one went hungry. Nevertheless, as the months had progressed, conditions and food had improved.

Those released were welcomed by the crowds at Galway Railway Station as conquering heroes. As they disembarked from the train, St Patrick's Band played the 'Soldiers' Song' as families, relatives and friends welcomed the men home. They were accompanied to their respective residences, temporary and permanent, by a torch-lit procession and a cheering, jubilant crowd. As Martin Crowe made his way home to Bohermore, he was led by the band playing national songs and followed by the enthusiastic crowd. Barrels of fire illuminated the streets and as he reached St Bridget's Terrace, almost opposite his home, the entire population of the street, men, women and children, gathered. Among the crowd were Peg Broderick, Seán Broderick, James Traynor and all his family, and the Folan family, including James. All remembered the suffering, hardship and loss that brought them to this conclusion.

The town and its population greeted all the other released prisoners in the same manner as they made their way home. Over seventy Galway men held prisoner in Rath Camp in the Curragh were also released the same week. The *Connacht Tribune* stated:

> In the annals of the historic City of the Tribes, seldom if ever before, was such an outburst of popular feeling witnessed as the demonstration which took place on Saturday night to celebrate the home-coming of political prisoners from Ballykinlar internment camp where they had undergone a long period of incarceration because they loved their native land.[7]

Many of the prisoners from south Galway were released from Rath Camp and travelled by train to Athenry. From there they were taken to Gort by motor transport. Bonfires lit the roadside in welcome and crowds gathered in the various villages to greet them. Among the released prisoners was James Carroll, who had been arrested with the Loughnane brothers.[8]

On 27 December 1921, the 17th Lancers from Earls Island held their farewell ball in the Town Hall. Guests arrived from various places around the country and the hall was elaborately decorated for the occasion. Their regimental dance took place the following evening, the last event for the Lancers in Galway.[9] The Lancers finally left Galway in February 1922 and travelled to North Wall in Dublin to sail to Liverpool and make their way to Tidworth. As they drove down the quay towards the steamer they were in a jovial mood, and raised their hats and shouted 'Goodbye Ireland!'[10]

On 2 February 1922, there was much celebration around Galway as the Black and Tans left on the 7 p.m. train en route for England. There was no pomp and ceremony – some said that the entire population was delighted to see them leave. While the Black and Tans had only been present a relatively short time, they left behind a legacy of hate that would not be easily forgotten. According to one newspaper report, this was the first time that the train crew were glad to see them on board, although they would have preferred if they had left by boat.[11] One by one the barracks in Galway county were vacated: Kilconnell, Dunmore, Headford, Tuam, Woodford. In Ballinasloe, the Tans sang 'God Save the King' as they began their journey for England.[12]

On 13 January 1922, the last of the republican prisoners

were released from Galway Jail. They included Thomas Kilroy and John Ryan, both from Caltra; Patrick Leahy and James Doorhy, both from Loughrea; and Patrick Coleman and Anthony Fallon, both from Ballina. As they emerged from the prison, they were greeted by members of the Prisoners' Committee and officers of the IRA and Cumann na mBan. The men were escorted to the tea rooms of P. O'Connor in Mainguard Street, where a reception was held for them.[13] That same day, the Auxiliaries at Lenaboy received two days' notice in which to pack up and leave Galway and return to England. The republican military authorities offered to purchase any stores that they could not take with them, for the right price.[14]

On Monday 13 February 1922, scenes of great enthusiasm greeted the takeover of Renmore Barracks by the IRA – members of A, B and C Companies of the Fourth Battalion were led into the post by the Industrial School Band. Earlier that morning, Commandant Seán Broderick and Adjutant Flaherty of the new Free State army had visited the barracks to view the evacuation preparations of the British Army. They had already taken over Lenaboy Castle from the Auxiliaries and made it their temporary headquarters. Captain Seán Turke took charge of the replacement of sentries at Renmore. The three senior officers then returned to Lenaboy to take charge of the companies and afterwards made their way back to Renmore Barracks. Large crowds attended the proceedings, and as the men marched through the entrance, a large tricolour was hoisted over the gate tower by an IRA officer. There was a huge cheer of excitement from the crowds and shouts of '*fáilte*'. The guard turned out fully equipped and presented arms as the battalion marched towards the parade ground. The men then gave a display of drill movements after which Divisional Commissioner Brennan inspected the building.[15]

The army left behind a number of military vehicles. However, the republicans were suspicious of these, worried that they may have been booby-trapped. Being a mechanic, Jim Furey was ordered to check them out. To his surprise, all were fully serviced and the log book and service records had been left with each vehicle.[16]

Epilogue

The War of Independence was a bitter conflict, fought by courageous men with little arms or training. Warfare for most of the IRA was part-time, and the men tried to live a normal life under difficult and sometimes dangerous circumstances. The danger from the Tans and Auxiliaries was ever-present and an encounter with these people could mean death or at least a severe beating. It was, for the most part, 'blood for blood without remorse', with little room for mercy. The events of the war shocked the British public, as news of murder, arson, torture, looting and systematic beatings of civilians spread. The Americans, who were well informed through the strong Irish network of organisations and immigrants, were also horrified, and pressure was brought to bear to bring about a cessation of the violence.

While the odds were against them, the IRA members fought back with increasing resolve and developed into a well-organised fighting force capable of meeting and defeating the Tans and Auxiliaries. They became as ruthless against informers as the Tans were against them. In areas where the republican courts and police were active, they were for the most part accepted by the people. However, by the time the Truce was signed in 1921, the IRA had virtually exhausted its military supplies. At any given time, it had no more than 2,000 men in the field, and as time went on it became extremely difficult to maintain even these numbers. Moreover, the country had been thrown into economic chaos by the ravages of the Tan war. There was a virtual cessation of railway traffic, brought about by the stubborn resistance of railway workers to transporting troops or munitions.

In 1920 the Government of Ireland Act had been brought in, envisaging a measure of Home Rule for both parts of a partitioned Ireland. It made provision for two parliaments in Ireland and, if agreed, a Council of Ireland was to be set up, which would be a law-making authority that would include both sides of the political divide. With the outcome of the Black and Tan war, this was not to be.[1]

The Irish people certainly proved, not just to Britain but also to the world, that they had a high tolerance for suffering. After all, this had been a legacy from their ancestors. Despite centuries of hardship and domination, each successive generation carried a deep love of Ireland, as was proved by the 1916 rebellion and its outcome. Not many people could have predicted the eventual outcome of these events, but the leaders must have realised the true yearning of the Irish soul for freedom. The men of 1916 displayed extraordinary courage when faced with the firing squad, and their last words are a testament to this commitment and bravery. The men who died and were executed during the War of Independence displayed similar courage and conviction.

Those who survived the War of Independence carried the scars for life. Some who had fought the British refused to pick up arms during the Civil War despite their beliefs, such as Sweeney Newell, who took no part. Perhaps his wounds prevented him from taking any further military action. In fact, it was seven weeks after his shooting in December 1920 before surgeons operated on him to remove the bullets and insert a plate into his hip. He remained in the George V Hospital until December 1921, when, along with four other former prisoners, he was transferred to the Mater Hospital. While in the Mater, he underwent thirteen additional operations, and it was May 1922 before he was finally released from hospital.[2] Newell suffered greatly from his wounds over the years. He lived in College Road, Galway, with his wife and children, until 1962, when he died of old age.

The statue of Lord Dunkellen, which had stood at Eyre Square since the 1860s, was pulled down following the signing of the Anglo-Irish Treaty. It was dragged through the streets of the town and thrown into the sea at Long Walk to the sound of a band playing 'I'm Forever Blowing Bubbles'. The plinth on which the statue had stood was later taken to Castlegar where it was used to support the IRA monument. The names of all the men who served with the Castlegar Brigade are recorded on the monument, except Sweeney Newell.

After the Civil War Jim Furey emigrated to the United States. Gretta Newell went ahead of him, but they had arranged to meet and were later married in Chicago. After a few years they returned to Ireland and lived in Ballybane, Galway. They had four children, but sadly Gretta and one of her babies died in a tragic house fire some years later.

James Traynor survived the Black and Tan war and took the Free State side in the Civil War. He died some time later from ill health, believed to have been caused by sleeping out in cemeteries and other such places while on the run. On the morning of his death his younger sister, Kitty, was nursing him. She always remembered the horror he went through on his deathbed as he relived the Black and Tan terror. She said that he pleaded with her a number of times to take 'the guns' from under his bed and hide them, as he could hear the Tans coming. There were no guns there, but to pacify him, she pretended that she had removed the weapons.

Following the Truce, Seán Broderick was appointed liaison officer under Michael Staines, who was later commissioner of the Garda Síochána.[3] Broderick married Kathleen O'Connor from Abbeygate Street in August 1934. They had three children, Pat, Michael and Valerie.[4]

Joe Togher fought on the Free State side during the Civil War and was almost killed twice. He became a captain in the new Irish army. After retiring from the military, he went back to work for the post office. He married Jenny Lydon from College Road and they had three children, Des, Tony and Bláth. Togher was an enthusiastic fisherman and later survived a tragic boating accident in which two of his friends lost their lives. He died in 1974 and was buried in Ross Errilly Abbey near Headford.[5]

Pat Margetts remained in Galway after the 'troubles' and married a Galway girl named Kathy Hill whose family had a shop in William Street. He became a prominent businessman and purchased Dillon's jewellery shop during the early 1920s. During the late 1950s his son John took over the business. John was joined by his son Jonathan during this period. The business moved to Quay Street in 1992 and today still trades under the management of Jonathan Margetts.[6]

Thomas 'Baby' Duggan fought with the Irregulars in the Civil War. Some say that he got the name 'Baby' because he was the youngest member of the Volunteers to turn out for the 1916 rebellion. He was captured by Free State troops at Rockwood in 1923 and taken to Galway Jail, and was subsequently sent to Newbridge, County Kildare, where he went on hunger strike for a time. He was released in 1924 along with other republican prisoners. However, his health was seriously affected, and shortly after returning to Galway he was taken to St Brides Home. His health continued to deteriorate slowly and he died on 12 February 1925 at just twenty-six years of age. The following is an extract from a tribute published at the time of his death.

> Though countless eyes are filled with tears,
> And loving hearts are sore;
> Those very hearts beat proudly;
> For the manly part he bore!

Poor Ireland has lost another of her dauntless and faithful sons; for her he lived, for her he worked, for her his health and strength were spent, and now for her he has died … It is sad to reflect that it was after incarceration at the hands of his own countrymen and former comrades-in-arms, his health completely broke down – in fact, he only came forth to die. O, the tragedy of it all. The man who laughed at danger, who had so many hair-breadth escapes, who carried supplies of arms to his harassed comrades under the very eyes of the Black and Tans, tracked down by his own, imprisoned, and let forth to die. Though he did more than a man's share in the fight for freedom, all too soon he has sunk to rest, his deeds of valour, his young life ended. May he rest in peace.[7]

In the years following the troubles, the country was torn politically and economically. Fianna Fáil was founded in 1926 after de Valera's secession from Sinn Féin.[8] In 1927 de Valera and the members of his new party abandoned their firm refusal to recognise the Irish Free State. They also took the oath of allegiance to the British king and with it their Dáil seats. Some of the old republicans refused to support them in this action.[9]

De Valera has been severely criticised for this, as his earlier refusal to accept the oath as part of the Treaty was one of the main causes of the Civil War.[10] However, he redeemed himself somewhat after winning the 1932 general election. On becoming taoiseach he contacted the British government and informed members that he intended to abolish the oath of allegiance. The British reacted by placing special duties on Irish imports to Britain, which they hoped would cripple Irish trade within six months. However, Ireland lasted out for almost six years, and the measures eventually became more damaging to Britain than to Ireland. By 1938 Britain had conceded to all of de Valera's demands, with the exception of the end of partition and full Irish independence. These were the vital points that led the Irish government to take a neutral stand during the Second World War.[11]

On Easter Monday, 18 April 1949, Ireland was declared a republic by John A. Costello. This had been signed into law the previous December and while Ulster remained separated from the twenty-six counties, the dream of the 1916 leaders had been at least partially realised. Possibly one of the most humiliating events for the British at that time was the removal of the statue of Queen Victoria from the courtyard of Leinster House.[12] Ireland was finally in control of her own destiny.

Appendix

Galway Roll of Honour

1916 Rebellion

Comdt Éamonn Ceannt, executed by crown forces in Kilmainham Jail, 8 May 1916

Brendan Donnellan, Loughrea, killed in action, South Dublin Union, 24 April 1916

War of Independence

Joseph Athy, Maree, killed by crown forces, 6 September 1920

Seán Mulvoy, Galway, killed by crown forces at Galway Railway Station, 8 September 1920

Seamus Quirke, Cork, killed by crown forces in Galway, 9 September 1920

John O'Hanlon, Turloughmore, killed by crown forces at home, 2 October 1920

Cllr Michael Walsh, Old Malt House, killed by crown forces in Galway, 20 October 1920

Thomas Egan, Coshla, killed by crown forces, 24 October 1920

Mrs Eileen Quinn, Lahane, killed by crown forces, 1 November 1920

Frank O'Dowd, Galway, died from the rigours of the struggle, 12 November 1920

Fr Michael Griffin, Gurteen, killed by crown forces in Galway, 14 November 1920

Michael Kildea, Woodlawn, killed by crown forces, 17 November 1920

William Cullinane, Lackagh, killed by crown forces, 21 November 1920

Comdt Michael Moran, Tuam, killed by crown forces, 24 November 1920

Patrick Loughnane, Shanaglish, killed by crown forces, 26 November 1920

Harry Loughnane, Shanaglish, killed by crown forces, 26 November 1920

Comdt Joseph Howley, Oranmore, killed by crown forces, 4 December 1920

Laurence MacDonagh, Oileain Arann, killed by crown forces, 23 December 1920

William Walsh, Headford, killed by crown forces, 18 January 1921

Jimmy Kirwan, Ballinastack, Ballygloonan, killed by crown forces, 21 January 1921

Michael Hoade, Caherlistrane, killed by crown forces, 21 January 1921

Thomas Collins, Headford, killed by crown forces, 22 January 1921

John Geoghegan, Magh Cuilinn, killed by crown forces, 20 February 1921

Thomas Mullen, Clonbern, killed by crown forces, March 1921

Thomas Whelan, Clifden, hanged in Mountjoy Jail, 14 March 1921

Louis D'Arcy, Headford, killed by crown forces, 24 March 1921

Patrick Cloonan, Maree, killed by crown forces, 5 April 1921

Thomas MacKeever, Dunmore, killed by crown forces, 2 May 1921

Hubert Tully, Clooneyquinn (Roscommon), killed by crown forces, 11 May 1921

Christopher Folan, Galway, killed by crown forces in Galway, 11 May 1921

Patrick Molloy, Kilroe, killed by crown forces, 1921

Thomas Ganley, Kilkerrin, killed by crown forces in Kilkerrin, 1921

Bill Freaney, Derrydonnell, killed in action near Athenry, 30 June 1921

James Keogh, Ballinasloe (date of death unknown)

James MacDonagh, Ballygar, killed in training, 1921

Paddy Halvey, Menlough, died a week after crown forces' beating, 1920/21

Michael Mullen, Moylough, killed by crown forces, 1920/21

Source: Daniel Callaghan, 2005

Notes

1. Rebellion in Galway

1   Henry, *Éamonn Ceannt*, pp. 135–6.

2   *Ibid.*

3   *Ibid.*, p. 91.

4   Ó Laoi, *The History of Castlegar Parish*, pp. 133–41.

2. Apostles of Freedom

1   Henry and O'Brien, *Galway's Great War Memorial Book 1914–1918*, p. 6.

2   Breen, *My Fight for Irish Freedom*, pp. 38–9, 64–6, 182–3.

3   Bennett, *The Black and Tans*, p. 25.

4   'The Apostles of Freedom Come to Galway', *Galway Express*, 17 May 1919.

3. Isolation and Danger

1   Ó Laoi, *The History of Castlegar Parish*, p. 142.

2   Witness Statement 1677: Seán Broderick, p. 2.

3   'Galway's Night of Terror in 1920', *Connacht Tribune*, 26 September 1920.

4   Witness Statement 1677: Seán Broderick, pp. 1–2.

5   Witness Statement 571: Michael Newell, pp. 2–3.

6   'Baton Charge', *Connacht Tribune*, 25 October 1919.

7   'N T and Tricolour', *Connacht Tribune*, 11 October 1919.

8   'Halt', *Connacht Tribune*, 31 January 1920.

9   'Dunmore Constable', *Connacht Tribune*, 24 January 1920.

10   'Galway Policeman', *Connacht Tribune*, 13 March 1920.

11   'Castlehacket Siege', *Connacht Tribune*, 17 January 1920.

12   Witness Statement, 1677: Seán Broderick, p. 3.

13   'Another Barracks Closed', *Connacht Tribune*, 27 February 1920.

14   'Night of Sensation', *Connacht Tribune*, 27 March 1920.

15   'Experience of a Sergeant's Wife', *Connacht Tribune*, 10 April 1920.

16   'Evacuated Constabulary Out-Post Burnt to the Ground', *Connacht Tribune*, 10 April 1920.

17   'Fighting in Flames', *Connacht Tribune*, 3 July 1920.

18   'Tyrone House Burnt', *Connacht Tribune*, 14 August 1920.

19   'Another Barracks Burnt', *Connacht Tribune*, 3 July 1920.

20   'In Full Retreat', *Connacht Tribune*, 24 July 1920.

21   'One Barrack Left', *Connacht Tribune*, 17 July 1920.

22   *Ibid.*

23   'Barracks Closed', *Connacht Tribune*, 24 January 1920.

24   'Portumna Surrounded', *Connacht Tribune*, 17 July 1920.

25   'To Disband Police', *Connacht Tribune*, 17 July 1920.

26   'Future of the R.I.C.', *Connacht Tribune*, 24 July 1920.

27   'Thinning the R.I.C. Ranks', *Connacht Tribune*, 14 August 1920.

4. Terrorising the Terrorists

1   'Shooting Affrays', *Connacht Tribune*, 24 January 1920.

2   'Letter-Box Raided – Mail-Car Robbed', *Connacht Tribune*, 10 April 1920.

3   'Lord Killanin Leaves Spiddal', *Connacht Tribune*, 28 February 1920.

4   'The Spiddal Prisoners', *Connacht Tribune*, 28 February 1920.

5   'Raid on Captain Barrett's Clonbur', *Connacht Tribune*, 28 February 1920.

6   'To Blow up a House', *Connacht Tribune*, 28 February 1920.

7   'J.P.'s Escape', *Connacht Tribune*, 1 May 1920.

8   'Shot Going to Mass', *Connacht Tribune*, 23 October 1920.

9   'Terrorising the Terrorists', *Connacht Tribune*, 21 January 1920.

10 'North Galway Tragedy', *Connacht Tribune*, 13 March 1920.

11 *Ibid.*

12 'Girl Sheared', *Connacht Tribune*, 3 May 1920.

13 'Shocking Outrages', *Connacht Tribune*, 7 August 1920.

14 'Volunteers Protect Public', *Connacht Tribune*, 31 July 1920.

5. The Arrival of the Black and Tans

1   Bennett, *The Black and Tans,* pp. 28, 30.

2   Margetts, 'I Remember', p. 5.

3   Quoted in the oration of Senator Mary White at Kilmichael, 26 November 2006.

4   'Khaki Policemen', *Connacht Tribune*, 28 February 1920.

5   Bennett, *The Black and Tans*, p. 28.

6   'Khaki Policemen', *Connacht Tribune*, 28 February 1920.

7   Interview: Amby Roche, 5 May 1999.

8   'Priests and Raids on Barracks', *Connacht Tribune*, 28 February 1920.

9   Bennett, *The Black and Tans*, p. 75.

10   www.historylearningsite.co.uk/black_and_tans.htm.

11   Witness Statement 1677: Seán Broderick, pp. 3–4.

12   'Drive to Death', *Connacht Tribune*, 6 March 1920.

13   'Woman Shot', *Connacht Tribune*, 23 October 1920.

14   'Escort Fired At', *Connacht Tribune*, 26 June 1920.

15   'Ardrahan Sergeant Ambushed', *Connacht Tribune*, 3 July 1920.

16   'Terrible Injuries', *Connacht Tribune*, 17 July 1920.

17   'Caltra Ambush', *Connacht Tribune*, 25 June 1920.

18   'Night of Sensation', *Connacht Tribune*, 27 March 1920.

19   'Military Lorry Smashed', *Connacht Tribune*, 26 June 1920.

20   'Arrests by Military', *Connacht Tribune*, 3 July 1920.

21   'Railway Hold Up', *Connacht Tribune*, 3 July 1920.

22   'No Road this Way!', *Connacht Tribune*, 26 June 1920.

6. Galway Hunger Strike

1   'Triumph After Ten Days', *Connacht Tribune*, 17 April 1920.

2   'Galway Prisoners', *Connacht Tribune*, 8 May 1920.

3   Interview: Kathleen Henry, 15 May 1975.

4   Coogan, *Michael Collins*, pp. 150–1.

7. Reprisals against Tuam

1   'Soldiers Open Fire', *Connacht Tribune*, 3 July 1920.

2   'A Dawn of Terror', *Connacht Tribune*, 24 July 1920.

3   Witness Statement 1246: Michael Cleary, p. 7.

4   'A Dawn of Terror', *Connacht Tribune*, 24 July 1920.

5   'A Truce of God', *Connacht Tribune*, 31 July 1920.

6   'A Dawn of Terror', *Connacht Tribune*, 24 July 1920.

7   'Tuam Terror', *Connacht Tribune*, 2 October 1920.

8   Witness Statement 1246: Michael Cleary, pp. 8–9.

9   Quoted in the oration of Senator Mary White at Kilmichael, 26 November 2006.

10   'Chief Sec. Speaks', *Connacht Tribune*, 2 October 1920.

8. The Merlin Park Ambush and Reprisal

1   Ó Laoi, *The History of Castlegar Parish*, pp. 142–3.

2   Furey, *The History of Oranmore Maree*, p. 64.

3   Ó Laoi, *The History of Castlegar Parish*, pp. 142–3.

4   'The Merlin Park Ambush', *Connacht Tribune*, 28 August 1920.

5   Ó Laoi, *The History of Castlegar Parish*, pp. 142–3.

6   'The Merlin Park Ambush', *Connacht Tribune*, 28 August 1920.

7   'The Sacking of Oranmore', *Galway Independent*, 22 February 2012.

8   'The Merlin Park Ambush', *Connacht Tribune*, 28 August 1920.

9   'Shots on the Street', *Connacht Tribune*, 28 August 1920.

10   'Last Night's Scenes', *Connacht Tribune*, 28 August 1920.

11   'The Sacking of Oranmore', *Galway Independent*, 22 February 2012.

12   'Sensational Tragedy', *Connacht Tribune*, 11 December 1920.

13   Furey, *The History of Oranmore Maree*, pp. 64–5.

14 'The Family Plight', *Connacht Tribune*, 28 August 1920.

15 Furey, *The History of Oranmore Maree*, pp. 64–5.

16 'The Sacking of Oranmore', *Galway Independent*, 22 February 2012.

17 'Air Force Officers and the Fire', *Connacht Tribune*, 28 August 1920.

18 'The War Upon the Police', *Connacht Tribune*, 28 August 1920.

19 Witness Statement 571: Michael Newell, p. 9.

9. Lancers Targeted

1 'Sinn Féin Aeroplanes', *Connacht Tribune*, 31 July 1920.

2 'Boycott of Police', *Connacht Tribune*, 31 July 1920.

3 O'Dowd, *Galway Lawn Tennis Club*, pp. 11–12.

4 Witness Statement 1677: Seán Broderick, p. 6.

5 'Shots in Galway', *Connacht Tribune*, 21 August 1920.

6 Ó Brolchain, *All in the Blood*, pp. 295–6.

7 Interview: Angela O'Toole and David Courtney, 7 August 2006.

8 'Military Evicted', *Connacht Tribune*, 21 August 1920.

10. Night of Terror

1 Margetts, 'I Remember', pp. 1–2.

2 Witness Statement 1677: Seán Broderick, p. 4.

3 'Military Inquest', *Connacht Tribune*, 18 September 1920.

4 'City's Night of Horror', *Connacht Tribune*, 11 September 1920.

5 Ó Laoi, 'Seán Turke', pp. 39–40.

6   Interview: Paddy O'Neill, 3 November 2005.

7   Interview: Martin Flaherty, 8 August 2011.

8   Ó Brolchain, *All in the Blood*, pp. 282–3.

9   'Galway Tragedies – The Military Inquest', *Connacht Tribune*, 18 September 1920.

10   Margetts, 'I Remember', p. 2.

11   'Galway's Night of Terror in 1920', *Connacht Tribune*, 26 September 1920.

12   Witness Statement 1677: Seán Broderick, pp. 5–6.

13   'Shop Assistant's Escape', *Connacht Tribune*, 11 September 1920.

14   'City's Night of Horror', *Connacht Tribune*, 11 September 1920.

15   'Military Inquest', *Connacht Tribune*, 18 September 1920.

16   Ó Brolchain, *All in the Blood*, pp. 282–3.

17   Margetts, 'I Remember', p. 2.

11. Funerals and Inquests

1   'Newspaper Office Wrecked', *Connacht Tribune*, 11 September 1920.

2   Ó Brolchain, *All in the Blood*, p. 284.

3   'Newspaper Office Wrecked', *Connacht Tribune*, 11 September 1920.

4   Margetts, 'I Remember', p. 2.

5   'Newspaper Office Wrecked', *Connacht Tribune*, 11 September 1920.

6   Margetts, 'I Remember', p. 3.

7   'To-Day's Funeral', *Connacht Tribune*, 11 September 1920.

8   Margetts, 'I Remember', 1929, p. 3.

9   'Quirke's Funeral', *Connacht Tribune*, 18 September 1920.

10   'To-Day's Funeral', *Connacht Tribune*, 11 September 1920.

11   'Military Inquest', *Connacht Tribune*, 18 September 1920. Cruise had only been in Galway a short time before violence broke out. His predecessor, District Inspector Hildebrand, seems to have had a better relationship with the people and more control over his men: Ó Brolchain, *All in the Blood*, pp. 281–2.

12   'Military Inquest', *Connacht Tribune*, 18 September 1920.

13   Margetts, 'I Remember', p. 4.

14   'Military Inquest', *Connacht Tribune*, 18 September 1920.

12. Terror Stalks the Streets

1   Margetts, 'I Remember', p. 6.

2   'City under Curfew', *Connacht Tribune*, 18 September 1920.

3   'Attack During Curfew Hours', *Connacht Tribune*, 30 October 1920.

4   Margetts, 'I Remember', pp. 4–5.

5   'City Under Curfew', *Connacht Tribune*, 18 September 1920.

6   'Girl's Allegation', *Connacht Tribune*, 2 October 1920.

7   'City Under Curfew', *Connacht Tribune*, 18 September 1920.

8   'Scene After Mass', *Connacht Tribune*, 2 October 1920.

9   'Mother's Screams,' *Connacht Tribune*, 30 October 1920.

10   Margetts, 'I Remember', p. 5.

11   Witness Statement 1682: Margaret 'Peg' Broderick-Nicholson, pp. 1–5.

12   'Ambush Victim', *Connacht Tribune*, 25 September 1920.

13 'R.I.C. Resignations', *Connacht Tribune*, 11 September 1920.

14 'Fictitious', *Connacht Tribune*, 2 October 1920.

13. Extended Tan Raids

1 'Ardrahan's Agony', *Connacht Tribune*, 2 October 1920.

2 'Scourged', *Connacht Tribune*, 23 October 1920.

3 'Three Men Shot', *Connacht Tribune*, 16 October 1920.

4 'Castledaly Ambush', *Connacht Tribune*, 6 November 1920.

5 'Mother Killed', *Connacht Tribune*, 6 November 1920.

6 'Horrible Outrage Near Gort: A Woman Killed with Child in her Arms', *The Galway Observer*, 6 November 1920.

7 'Mother Killed', *Connacht Tribune*, 6 November 1920.

8 'Horrible Outrage Near Gort: A Woman Killed with Child in her Arms', *The Galway Observer*, 6 November 1920.

14. Singled Out for Murder

1 Interview: William O'Hanlon and Dick O'Hanlon, 20 July 2010.

2 Blackmore, Cronin, Ferrie and Higgins (eds), *In Their Own Words*, pp. 207–9.

3 'Five Police were Surrounded and their Bicycles and Capes were Taken', *Dublin Evening Mail*, 28 June 1920.

4 Interview: Dick O'Hanlon, 20 March 2011.

5 'Priest Arrested', *Connacht Tribune*, 9 October 1920.

6 'Mass House Entered', *Connacht Tribune*, 23 October 1920.

7 'Oranmore Men Shot', *Connacht Tribune*, 23 October 1920.

8 'Coshla Crime', *Connacht Tribune*, 30 October 1920.

15. Murder at Long Walk

1 'The Raid on the Old Malt House', *Connacht Tribune*, 25 September 1920.

2 Ó Laoi, *Fr Griffin 1892–1920*, p. 35.

3 Interview: Tom Joe Furey, 20 May 2006.

4 'City Horror', *Connacht Tribune*, 23 October 1920.

5 Interview: Mary O'Brien, 4 October 2006.

6 'City Horror', *Connacht Tribune*, 23 October 1920.

7 'Set On Fire', *Connacht Tribune*, 30 October 1920.

8 'City Raids', *Connacht Tribune*, 30 October 1920.

16. Intelligence Operations

1 Witness Statement 1729: Joseph Togher, pp. 1–4.

2 Ó Laoi, *Fr Griffin 1892–1920*, p. 67.

3 Witness Statement 1729: Joseph Togher, pp. 1–4.

4 'Teacher Kidnapped', *Connacht Tribune*, 23 October 1920.

5 Ó Laoi, *Fr Griffin 1892–1920*, pp. 28–9, 67–70.

6 Witness Statement 1729: Joseph Togher, pp. 5–6.

7 Interview: Pascal Spelman, 6 March 2003.

17. The Murder of Fr Griffin

1 Ó Laoi, *Fr Griffin 1892–1920*, pp. 5, 18–19, 22, 30–2.

2 Ó Brolchain, *All in the Blood*, pp. 193–4.

3 Ó Laoi, *Fr Griffin 1892–1920*, pp. 33–8, 43.

4 'Murder of Fr Griffin', *The Galway Observer*, 27 November 1920.

5 Ó Laoi, *Fr Griffin 1892–1920*, pp. 42–3, 50.

6 Interview: Kathleen Henry, 15 May 1975.

7 Ó Laoi, *Fr Griffin 1892–1920*, p. 61.

8 'Fr Griffin's Murder was Reprisal for Dead Spy', *Galway Advertiser*, 7 April 1994.

9 Witness Statement 1729: Joseph Togher, pp. 8–9.

10 'A Spent Bullet One Dark November Night', *Galway Advertiser*, 21 November 2002.

11 Margetts, 'I Remember', p. 9.

12 Witness Statement 1126: Michael Francis Kelly-Mor, p. 1.

13 Interview: Pat Dolan, 5 May 2011.

14 Jackson (ed.) and Greaves, *Ireland Her Own*, p. 419.

18. Murder of the Loughnane Brothers

1 'Mystery of how Brothers Died', *Connacht Tribune*, 11 December 1920.

2 Witness Statement 1334: Joseph Stanford, p. 3.

3 'Horrific Death of Brothers at Hands of Black and Tans', *An Phoblacht Republican News*, 7 December 2000.4

4 'Mystery of how Brothers Died', *Connacht Tribune*, 11 December 1920.

5 'Horrific Death of Brothers at Hands of Black and Tans', *An Phoblacht Republican News*, 7 December 2000.

6 'Mystery of how Brothers Died', *Connacht Tribune*, 11 December 1920.

7 'Horrific Death of Brothers at Hands of Black and Tans', *An Phoblacht Republican News*, 7 December 2000.

8 'Mystery of how Brothers Died', *Connacht Tribune*, 11 December 1920.

9   'Dream Reveals Murder', *Connacht Tribune*, 15 October 1920.

10 'Mystery of how Brothers Died', *Connacht Tribune*, 11 December 1920.

11 'Horrific Death of Brothers at Hands of Black and Tans', *An Phoblacht Republican News*, 7 December 2000.

12 'Mystery of how Brothers Died', *Connacht Tribune*, 11 December 1920.

13 'The Truce of God', *Connacht Tribune*, 11 December 1920.

14 Margetts, 'I Remember', p. 7.

15 'No Further Accommodation', *Connacht Tribune*, 11 December 1920.

16 'Galway Workhouse Raided', *Connacht Tribune*, 11 December 1920.

17 'City Arrests', *Connacht Tribune*, 1920.

19. Dublin Shootings and Aran Island Raids

1   Furey, *The History of Oranmore Maree*, p. 65.

2   'Sensational Tragedy', *Connacht Tribune*, 11 December 1920.

3   'Commdt. Joe Howley', *Connacht Tribune*, 11 December 1970.

4   Furey, *The History of Oranmore Maree*, p. 65.

5   Witness Statement 1729: Joseph Togher, pp. 3–4.

6   Witness Statement 698: Thomas Newell, pp. 6–7.

7   Witness Statement 1729: Joseph Togher, pp. 3–4.

8   Pudon, *The War of Independence*, pp. 52–3.

9   'Peace Hopes', *Connacht Tribune*, 11 December 1920.

10 'Peace in Ireland', *Connacht Tribune*, 4 December 1920.

11 'Christmas Truce', *Connacht Tribune*, 4 December 1920.

12 'Island Tragedy', *Connacht Tribune*, 25 December 1920.

13 'When the British Tried to Invade the Aran Islands', *Galway Advertiser*, 24 September 2009.

14 'Island Tragedy', *Connacht Tribune*, 25 December 1920.

15 'Died in Prison', *Connacht Tribune*, 3 January 1921.

16 Ó Brolchain, *All in the Blood*, pp. 282–3, 299.

17 Interview: Bridget Dirrane, 3 April 1998. She later wrote *A Woman of Aran* when she was over 100 years of age.

20. Ambush and Aftermath

1 Witness Statement 571: Michael Newell, pp. 7–8.

2 'Ambush and Tragic Aftermath', *Connacht Tribune*, 22 January 1921.

3 'A Mother's Woe', *Connacht Tribune*, 9 July 1921.

4 'Three Men Shot Dead', *Connacht Tribune*, 22 January 1921.

5 'Bomb Shatters Bar', *Connacht Tribune*, 5 February 1921.

6 'Miss Alice Cashel', *Connacht Tribune*, 26 February 1921.

7 'House Burnings', *Connacht Tribune*, 12 February 1921.

8 'Midnight Blaze', *Connacht Tribune*, 19 February 1921.

9 'County Councillors' Houses Bombed', *Connacht Tribune*, 19 February 1921.

10 'Cheery Prisoners', *Connacht Tribune*, 19 February 1921.

11 Margetts, 'I Remember', pp. 7–9.

21. Clifden Attacked

1 One of the three-man party who had carried out the killing

of Baggallay was Seán Lemass, a future taoiseach of Ireland. Coogan, *Michael Collins*, p. 159.

2   'Clifden's Thomas Whelan to be Buried with Kevin Barry on Sunday', *Galway Advertiser*, 11 October 2001.

3   Villiers-Tuthill, *Beyond the Twelve Bens*, pp. 202–4.

4   'T. Whelan's Fate', *Connacht Tribune*, 12 March 1921.

5   Villiers-Tuthill, *Beyond the Twelve Bens*, pp. 206, 208.

6   'Clifden's Thomas Whelan to be Buried with Kevin Barry on Sunday', *Galway Advertiser*, 11 October 2001.

7   Villiers-Tuthill, *Beyond the Twelve Bens*, p. 206.

8   *Ibid.*, pp. 208–11.

9   'The Night the Tans Burnt Clifden', *Galway Advertiser*, 4 May 2006.

10 Villiers-Tuthill, *Beyond the Twelve Bens*, p. 212.

11 'Death and Destruction in Clifden', *Connacht Tribune*, 26 March 1921.

12 *Ibid.*

13 Villiers-Tuthill, *Beyond the Twelve Bens*, p. 212.

22. Terror on Both Sides

1   Furey, *The History of Oranmore Maree*, pp. 64–6.

2   Ó Brolchain, *All in the Blood*, pp. 300, 303.

3   Interview: Padraig Kavanagh, 30 October 2011.

4   'Old Galway', *Galway Advertiser*, 25 January 1986.

5   Witness Statement 298: Alf Monahan, p. 5.

6   'Old Galway', *Galway Advertiser*, 25 January 1986.

7   'General Tudor in Galway', *Connacht Tribune*, 9 April 1921.

8   'Ghastly Find', *Connacht Tribune*, 9 April 1921.

9   'Kinvara Tragedy', *Connacht Tribune*, 9 April 1921.

10 'R.I.C. Men Wounded', *Connacht Tribune*, 23 April 1921.

11 'Midnight Terror at Milltown', *Connacht Tribune*, 15 October 1921.

12 'Killed Outright', *Connacht Tribune*, 2 July 1921.

13 'Shot from Thicket', *Connacht Tribune*, 9 April 1921.

14 'Mountain Battle', *Connacht Tribune*, 30 April 1921.

15 'Ambush – and After', *Connacht Tribune*, 21 May 1921.

16 Witness Statement 453: George Staunton, p. 17.

17 'Unknown Persons', *Connacht Tribune*, 7 May 1921.

18 'Headford Attack', *Connacht Tribune*, 7 May 1921.

19 'Ambush at Dunmore', *Connacht Tribune*, 7 May 1921.

23. Terror in the Terrace

1   'Remembering Hubert Tully', *Galway Advertiser*, 9 May 1996.

2   'Double Tragedy', *Connacht Tribune*, 14 May 1921.

3   Witness Statement 1677: Seán Broderick, pp. 3–4.

4   'Double Tragedy', *Connacht Tribune*, 14 May 1921. The bullet passed through and lodged in the timber of the stairs. It was never removed and today it is covered with a gold cross. The house is now owned by Mary Kate Fahy.

5   Interview: Kathleen Henry, 15 May 1975.

6   Interview: Mark Kennedy, 6 June 2006.

7   Interview: Paddy O'Neill, 3 November 2005.

8   Interview: Tom Joe Furey, 20 May 2006.

9   'Are You Dead?', *Connacht Tribune*, 21 May 1921.

10 'Beaten and Shot', *Connacht Tribune*, 3 September 1921.

24. Final Actions

1   'Seán Broderick and the Black and Tans', *Galway Advertiser*, 9 April 2009.

2   Interview: Tom Small, 10 May 2006.

3   Interview: Angela O'Toole and David Courtney, 5 June 2006.

4   'Joe Togher, a Galway Volunteer', *Galway Advertiser*, 9 April 2009.

5   'Died Together', *Connacht Tribune*, 21 May 1921.

6   'Gort Ambush', *Connacht Tribune*, 28 May 1921.

7   'Died Together', *Connacht Tribune*, 21 May 1921.

8   Witness Statement 1334: Joseph Stanford, pp. 44, 46.

9   'Ten Shots', *Connacht Tribune*, 11 June 1921.

10 'Awards £200,000', *Connacht Tribune*, 2 July 1921.

11 'Cadets Claim £12,000', *Connacht Tribune*, 2 July 1921.

12 'Charred Remains', *Connacht Tribune*, 2 July 1921.

13 'The Last Shots', *Connacht Tribune*, 16 July 1921.

25. The Dawn of Freedom

1   'The West Rejoices', *Connacht Tribune*, 16 July 1921.

2   Pudon, *The War of Independence*, pp. 54–8.

3   Neeson, *The Civil War in Ireland 1922–1923*, pp. 52–3.

4   'Deplorable Tragedy', *Connacht Tribune*, 8 October 1921.

5   'Dramatic Protest', *Connacht Tribune*, 26 November 1921.

6   'No Surrender', *Connacht Tribune*, 12 November 1921.

7   'The Home Coming', *Connacht Tribune*, 17 December 1921.

8   'Captivity to Freedom', *Connacht Tribune*, 17 December 1921.

9 'Lancers' Farewell Dance', *Connacht Tribune*, 31 December 1921. It is interesting to note that their farewell ball took place at the same venue as the prisoners' relief fund ceilidh almost three months earlier.

10 '17th Lancers Good-bye to Ireland', *Connacht Tribune*, 18 February 1922.

11 'Black and Tans Leave', *Connacht Tribune*, 4 February 1922.

12 'Barracks Evacuated', *Connacht Tribune*, 4 February 1922.

13 'Freedom', *Connacht Tribune*, 14 January 1922.

14 'Auxiliaries Under Orders to Leave', *Connacht Tribune*, 14 January 1922.

15 'Irishmen Receive Surrender of Renmore Depot', *Connacht Tribune*, 18 February 1922.

16 Interview: Tom Joe Furey, 20 May 2006.

Epilogue

1 Jackson (ed.) and Greaves, *Ireland Her Own*, pp. 414–19.

2 Witness Statement 572: Thomas Newell, pp. 6–7.

3 Witness Statement 1677: Seán Broderick, p. 6.

4 'Seán Broderick and the Black and Tans', *Galway Advertiser*, 9 April 2009.

5 'Joe Togher, a Galway Volunteer', *Galway Advertiser*, 9 April 2009.

6 'Dillon's of Galway', *Galway Independent*, 1 December 2010.

7 'Former I.R.A. Commandant', *Connacht Tribune*, 14 February 1925.

8 Foster, *The Oxford Illustrated History of Ireland*, p. 257.

9 Jackson (ed.) and Greaves, *Ireland Her Own*, p. 428.

10 Ó Gadhra, *Civil War in Connacht 1922–1923*, p. 82.

11 Jackson (ed.) and Greaves, *Ireland Her Own*, p. 429.

12 Foster, *The Oxford Illustrated History of Ireland*, pp. 266, 269.

Bibliography

Documents

Oration of Senator Mary White at Kilmichael, 26 November 2006

Pat Margetts, 'I Remember: The Experiences and Adventures of one of the Crown Forces during the Anglo-Irish Struggle of 1920–21', Galway 1929

Eleven Galway Martyrs, 1985

Interviews

Bridget Dirrane, 3 April 1998

Pat Dolan, 5 May 2011

Martin Flaherty, 8 August 2011

Tom Joe Furey, 20 May 2006

Kathleen Henry, 15 May 1975

Padraig Kavanagh, 30 October 2011

Mark Kennedy, 6 June 2006

Mary O'Brien, 4 October 2006

Dick O'Hanlon, 20 March 2011

William O'Hanlon and Dick O'Hanlon, 20 July 2010

Paddy O'Neill, 3 November 2005

Angela O'Toole and David Courtney, 7 August 2006

Amby Roche, 5 May 1999

Tom Small, 10 May 2006

Pascal Spelman, 6 March 2003

Newspaper Articles

'17th Lancers Good-bye to Ireland', *Connacht Tribune*, 18 February 1922

'A Dawn of Terror', *Connacht Tribune*, 24 July 1920

'Air Force Officers and the Fire', *Connacht Tribune*, 28 August 1920

'Ambush – and After', *Connacht Tribune*, 21 May 1921

'Ambush and Tragic Aftermath', *Connacht Tribune*, 22 January 1921

'Ambush at Dunmore', *Connacht Tribune*, 7 May 1921

'Ambush Victim', *Connacht Tribune*, 25 September 1920

'A Mother's Woe', *Connacht Tribune*, 9 July 1921

'Another Barracks Burnt', *Connacht Tribune*, 3 July 1920

'Another Barracks Closed', *Connacht Tribune*, 27 February 1920

'Ardrahan's Agony', *Connacht Tribune*, 2 October 1920

'Ardrahan Sergeant Ambushed', *Connacht Tribune*, 3 July 1920

'Are You Dead?', *Connacht Tribune*, 21 May 1921

'Arrests by Military', *Connacht Tribune*, 3 July 1920

'A Spent Bullet One Dark November Night', *Galway Advertiser*, 21 November 2002

'A Truce of God', *Connacht Tribune*, 31 July 1920

'Attack During Curfew Hours', *Connacht Tribune*, 30 October 1920

'Auxiliaries Under Orders to Leave', *Connacht Tribune*, 14 January 1922

'Awards £200,000', *Connacht Tribune*, 2 July 1921

'Barracks Closed', *Connacht Tribune*, 24 January 1920

'Barracks Evacuated', *Connacht Tribune*, 4 February 1922

'Baton Charge', *Connacht Tribune*, 25 October 1919

'Beaten and Shot', *Connacht Tribune*, 3 September 1921

'Black and Tans Leave', *Connacht Tribune*, 4 February 1922

'Bohermore Ambush', *Connacht Tribune*, 13 January 1923

'Bomb Shatters Bar', *Connacht Tribune*, 5 February 1921

'Boycott of Police', *Connacht Tribune*, 31 July 1920

'Cadets Claim £12,000', *Connacht Tribune*, 2 July 1921

'Caltra Ambush', *Connacht Tribune*, 25 June 1920

'Captivity To Freedom', *Connacht Tribune*, 17 December 1921

'Castledaly Ambush', *Connacht Tribune*, 6 November 1920

'Castlehacket Siege', *Connacht Tribune*, 17 January 1920

'Charred Remains', *Connacht Tribune*, 2 July 1921

'Cheery Prisoners', *Connacht Tribune*, 19 February 1921

'Chief Sec. Speaks', *Connacht Tribune*, 2 October 1920

'Christmas Truce', *Connacht Tribune*, 4 December 1920

'City Arrests', *Connacht Tribune*, 1920

'City Horror', *Connacht Tribune*, 23 October 1920

'City's Night of Horror', *Connacht Tribune*, 11 September 1920

'City Raids', *Connacht Tribune*, 30 October 1920

'City Under Curfew', *Connacht Tribune*, 18 September 1920

'Clifden's Thomas Whelan to be buried with Kevin Barry on
    Sunday', *Galway Advertiser*, 11 October 2001

'Co. Flying Column', *Connacht Tribune*, 24 February 1923

'Commdt. Joe Howley', *Connacht Tribune*, 11 December 1970

'Coshla Crime', *Connacht Tribune*, 30 October 1920

'County Councillors' Houses Bombed', *Connacht Tribune*, 19
    February 1921

'Death and Destruction in Clifden', *Connacht Tribune*, 26 March
    1921

'Deplorable Tragedy', *Connacht Tribune*, 8 October 1921

'Died in Prison', *Connacht Tribune*, 3 January 1921

'Died Together', *Connacht Tribune*, 21 May 1921

'Dillon's of Galway', *Galway Independent*, 1 December 2010

'Double Tragedy', *Connacht Tribune*, 14 May 1921

'Dramatic Protest', *Connacht Tribune*, 26 November 1921

'Dream Reveals Murder', *Connacht Tribune*, 15 October 1920

'Drive to Death', *Connacht Tribune*, 6 March 1920

'Dunmore Constable', *Connacht Tribune*, 24 January 1920

'Eglinton St. Barracks Burned – Also Renmore Barracks and
    Naval Base', *The Galway Observer*, 8 July 1922

'Escort Fired At', *Connacht Tribune*, 26 June 1920

'Evacuated Constabulary Out-Post Burnt to the Ground', *Connacht Tribune*, 10 April 1920

'Executed – Six County Galway Men Suffered Death Penalty –
    Natives of Headford – Confined in Galway Jail until Tuesday', *Connacht Tribune*, 14 April 1923

'Experience of a Sergeant's Wife', *Connacht Tribune*, 10 April
    1920

'Fictitious', *Connacht Tribune*, 2 October 1920

'Fighting in Flames', *Connacht Tribune*, 3 July 1920

'Five Police were Surrounded and their Bicycles and Capes were
    Taken', *Dublin Evening Mail*, 28 June 1920

'Former I.R.A. Commandant', *Connacht Tribune*, 14 February
    1925

'Fr Griffin's Murder was Reprisal for Dead Spy', *Galway Advertiser*, 7 April 1994

'Freedom', *Connacht Tribune*, 14 January 1922

'Future of the RIC', *Connacht Tribune*, 24 July 1920

'Galway Policeman', *Connacht Tribune*, 13 March 1920

'Galway Prisoners', *Connacht Tribune*, 8 May 1920

'Galway Tragedies – The Military Inquest', *Connacht Tribune*, 18 September 1920

'Galway Workhouse Raided', *Connacht Tribune*, 11 December 1920

'Galway's Night of Terror in 1920', *Connacht Tribune*, 26 September 1920

'Ghastly Find', *Connacht Tribune*, 9 April 1921

'General Tudor in Galway', *Connacht Tribune*, 9 April 1921

'Girl Sheared', *Connacht Tribune*, 3 May 1920

'Girl's Allegation', *Connacht Tribune*, 2 October 1920

'Gort Ambush', *Connacht Tribune*, 28 May 1921

'Halt', *Connacht Tribune*, 31 January 1920

'Headford Attack', *Connacht Tribune*, 7 May 1921

'Horrible Outrage Near Gort: A Woman Killed with Child in her Arms', *The Galway Observer*, 6 November 1920

'Horrific Death of Brothers at Hands of Black and Tans', *An Phoblacht Republican News*, 7 December 2000

'House Burnings', *Connacht Tribune*, 12 February 1921

'In Full Retreat', *Connacht Tribune*, 24 July 1920

'Incidents In Tuam', *Galway Advertiser*, 19 August 1999

'Irishmen Receive Surrender of Renmore Depot', *Connacht Tribune*, 18 February 1922

'Island Tragedy', *Connacht Tribune*, 25 December 1920

'J.P.'s Escape', *Connacht Tribune*, 1 May 1920

'Joe Togher, a Galway Volunteer', *Galway Advertiser*, 9 April 2009

'Khaki Policemen', *Connacht Tribune*, 28 February 1920

'Killed Outright', *Connacht Tribune*, 2 July 1921

'Kinvara Tragedy', *Connacht Tribune*, 9 April 1921

'Last Night's Scenes', *Connacht Tribune*, 28 August 1920

'Lancers Farewell Dance', *Connacht Tribune*, 31 December 1921

'Letter-Box Raided – Mail-Car Robbed', *Connacht Tribune*, 10 April 1920

'Lord Killanin Leaves Spiddal', *Connacht Tribune*, 28 February 1920

'Mass House Entered', *Connacht Tribune*, 23 October 1920

'Midnight Blaze', *Connacht Tribune*, 19 February 1921

'Midnight Terror at Milltown', *Connacht Tribune*, 15 October 1921

'Miles of Mourners', *Connacht Tribune*, 3 February 1923

'Military Evicted', *Connacht Tribune*, 21 August 1920

'Military Inquest', *Connacht Tribune*, 18 September 1920

'Military Lorry Smashed', *Connacht Tribune*, 26 June 1920

'Miss Alice Cashel', *Connacht Tribune*, 26 February 1921

'Mother Killed', *Connacht Tribune*, 6 November 1920

'Mother's Screams', *Connacht Tribune*, 30 October 1920

'Mountain Battle', *Connacht Tribune*, 30 April 1921

'Murder of Fr Griffin', *The Galway Observer*, 27 November 1920

'Mystery of how Brothers Died', *Connacht Tribune*, 11 December 1920

'Newspaper Office Wrecked', *Connacht Tribune*, 11 September 1920

'Night of Sensation', *Connacht Tribune*, 27 March 1920

'No Further Accommodation', *Connacht Tribune*, 11 December 1920

'No Road this Way!', *Connacht Tribune*, 26 June 1920

'No Surrender', *Connacht Tribune*, 12 November 1921

'North Galway Tragedy', *Connacht Tribune*, 13 March 1920

'N T and Tricolour', *Connacht Tribune*, 11 October 1919

'Old Galway', *Galway Advertiser*, 25 January 1986

'One Barrack Left', *Connacht Tribune*, 17 July 1920

'Oranmore Men Shot', *Connacht Tribune*, 23 October 1920

'Peace Hopes', *Connacht Tribune*, 11 December 1920

'Peace in Ireland', *Connacht Tribune*, 4 December 1920

'Portumna Surrounded', *Connacht Tribune*, 17 July 1920

'Priest Arrested', *Connacht Tribune*, 9 October 1920

'Priests and Raids on Barracks', *Connacht Tribune*, 28 February 1920

'Quirke's Funeral', *Connacht Tribune*, 18 September 1920

'Raid on Captain Barrett's Clonbur', *Connacht Tribune*, 28 February 1920

'Railway Hold Up', *Connacht Tribune*, 3 July 1920

'Remembering Hubert Tully', *Galway Advertiser*, 9 May 1996

'R.I.C. Men Wounded', *Connacht Tribune*, 23 April 1921

'R.I.C. Resignations', *Connacht Tribune*, 11 September 1920

'Scene After Mass', *Connacht Tribune*, 2 October 1920

'Scourged', *Connacht Tribune*, 23 October 1920

'Seán Broderick and the Black and Tans', *Galway Advertiser*, 9 April 2009

'Sensational Tragedy', *Connacht Tribune*, 11 December 1920

'Set On Fire', *Connacht Tribune*, 30 October 1920

'Shades of the Wild West and War', *Galway Advertiser*, 22 February 2007

'Shocking Outrages', *Connacht Tribune*, 7 August 1920

'Shop Assistant's Escape', *Connacht Tribune*, 11 September 1920

'Shooting Affrays', *Connacht Tribune*, 24 January 1920

'Shot from Thicket', *Connacht Tribune*, 9 April 1921

'Shot Going to Mass', *Connacht Tribune*, 23 October 1920

'Shots in Galway', *Connacht Tribune*, 21 August 1920

'Shots on the Street', *Connacht Tribune*, 28 August 1920

'Sinn Féin Aeroplanes', *Connacht Tribune*, 31 July 1920

'Soldiers Open Fire', *Connacht Tribune*, 3 July 1920

'T. Whelan's Fate', *Connacht Tribune*, 12 March 1921

'Teacher Kidnapped', *Connacht Tribune*, 23 October 1920

'Ten Shots', *Connacht Tribune*, 11 June 1921

'Terrible Injuries', *Connacht Tribune*, 17 July 1920

'Terrorising the Terrorists', *Connacht Tribune*, 21 January 1920

'The Apostles of Freedom come to Galway', *Galway Express*, 17 May 1919

'The Chief of Staff, IRA', *Connacht Tribune*, 21 December 1921

'The Family Plight', *Connacht Tribune*, 28 August 1920

'The Home Coming', *Connacht Tribune*, 17 December 1921

'The Last Shots', *Connacht Tribune*, 16 July 1921

'The Merlin Park Ambush', *Connacht Tribune*, 28 August 1920

'The Night the Tans burnt Clifden', *Galway Advertiser*, 4 May 2006

'The Peace Terms', *Connacht Tribune*, 20 August 1921

'The Raid on the Old Malt House', *Connacht Tribune*, 25 September 1920

'The Sacking of Oranmore', *Galway Independent*, 22 February 2012

'The Spiddal Prisoners', *Connacht Tribune*, 28 February 1920

'The Truce of God', *Connacht Tribune*, 11 December 1920

'The War Upon the Police', *Connacht Tribune*, 28 August 1920

'The West Rejoices', *Connacht Tribune*, 16 July 1921

'Thinning the R.I.C. Ranks', *Connacht Tribune*, 14 August 1920

'Three Men Shot', *Connacht Tribune*, 16 October 1920

'Three Men Shot Dead', *Connacht Tribune*, 22 January 1921

'To Blow up a House', *Connacht Tribune*, 28 February 1920

'To-Day's Funeral', *Connacht Tribune*, 11 September 1920

'To Disband Police', *Connacht Tribune*, 17 July 1920

'Triumph After Ten Days', *Connacht Tribune*, 17 April 1920

'Tuam Terror', *Connacht Tribune*, 2 October 1920

'Tyrone House Burnt', *Connacht Tribune*, 14 August 1920

'Unknown Persons', *Connacht Tribune*, 7 May 1921

'Volunteers Protect Public', *Connacht Tribune*, 31 July 1920

'When the British Tried to Invade the Aran Islands', *Galway Advertiser*, 24 September 2009

'Woman Shot', *Connacht Tribune*, 23 October 1920

Witness Statements

Witness Statement 1677: Seán Broderick

Witness Statement 1682: Margaret 'Peg' Broderick-Nicholson

Witness Statement 1246: Michael Cleary

Witness Statement 1126: Michael Francis Kelly-Mor

Witness Statement 298: Alf Monahan (Ailbhe Ó Monacháin)

Witness Statement 571: Michael Newell

Witness Statement 572, 698: Thomas Newell

Witness Statement 1334: Joseph Stanford

Witness Statement 453: George Staunton

Witness Statement 1729: Joseph Togher

Secondary Sources

Bennett, R., *The Black and Tans* (London: New English Library Limited, 1970)

Blackmore, L., Cronin, J., Ferrie, D. and Higgins, B. (eds), *In Their Own Words* (Galway: Lackagh Museum Committee, 2001)

Breen, D., *My Fight for Irish Freedom* (Kerry: Anvil, 1975)

Coogan, T. P., *Michael Collins: A Biography* (London: Hutchinson, 1990)

——, *De Valera: Long Fellow, Long Shadow* (London: Hutchinson, 1993)

Foster, R. F., *The Oxford Illustrated History of Ireland* (Oxford: Oxford University Press, 1989)

Furey, B., *The History of Oranmore Maree* (Galway: Brenda Furey, 1991)

Henry, W., *Éamonn Ceannt: Supreme Sacrifice* (Cork: Mercier Press, 2012)

—— and O'Brien, J., *Galway's Great War Memorial Book 1914–1918* (Galway: Galway City Council, 2007)

Hopkins, M., *Green Against Green: The Irish Civil War* (Dublin: Gill & Macmillan, 1988)

Jackson, T. A. (ed.) and C. Desmond Greaves, *Ireland Her Own: An Outline History of the Irish Struggle* (New York: International Publishers, 1973)

Litton, H., *The Irish Civil War: An Illustrated History* (Dublin: Wolfhound Press, 2001)

Neeson, E., *The Civil War in Ireland 1922–1923* (Cork: Mercier Press, 1989)

Ó Brolchain, H., *All in the Blood: A Memoir by Geraldine Plunkett Dillon* (Dublin: A & A Farmar Ltd, 2006)

O'Dowd, P., *Galway Lawn Tennis Club: A History* (Galway: Galway Lawn Tennis Club, 2005)

Ó Gadhra, N., *Civil War in Connacht 1922–1923* (Cork: Mercier Press, 1999)

Ó Laoi, P., 'Seán Turke', *St Patrick's Parish Magazine*, 1980–81

——, *Fr Griffin 1892–1920* (Galway: Pádraic Ó Laoi, 1994)

——, *The History of Castlegar Parish* (Galway: Pádraic Ó Laoi, 1998)

O'Malley, E., *The Singing Flame* (Cork: Mercier Press, 2012)

Pudon, E., *The War of Independence* (Cork: Mercier Press, 2001)

Villiers-Tuthill, K., *Beyond the Twelve Bens: A History of Clifden and District 1860–1923* (Galway: Kathleen Villiers-Tuthill, 1990)

Index

By the Same Author